THE BEAUTIFUL RISK OF EDUCATION

Interventions: Education, Philosophy, and Culture

Edited by Michael A. Peters

THE BEAUTIFUL RISK
OF EDUCATION

Gert J. J. Biesta

Paradigm Publishers
Boulder • London

Copyright © 2013 by Paradigm Publishers

Published in the United States by Paradigm Publishers, 5589 Arapahoe Avenue, Boulder, CO 80303 USA.

Paradigm Publishers is the trade name of Birkenkamp & Company, LLC, Dean Birkenkamp, President and Publisher.

Library of Congress Cataloging-in-Publication Data

Biesta, Gert, author.
 The beautiful risk of education / Gert J. J. Biesta.
    pages cm. — (Interventions: education, philosophy, and culture)
 Includes bibliographical references and index.
 ISBN 978-1-61205-026-3 (hardcover : alk. paper)
 ISBN 978-1-61205-027-0 (pbk. : alk. paper)
 1. Education—Philosophy. 2. Education—Aims and objectives. 3. Teaching—Philosophy. I. Title.
 LB14.7.B527 2012
 370.1—dc23

                                                                                2012043666

Printed and bound in the United States of America on acid-free paper that meets the standards of the American National Standard for Permanence of Paper for Printed Library Materials.

Designed and Typeset in Adobe Garamond by Straight Creek Bookmakers.

17 16 15 14 13   1 2 3 4 5

One has to accept that "it" [ça] (the other, or whatever "it" may be) is stronger than I am, for something to happen. I have to lack a certain strength, I have to lack it enough, for something to happen. If I were stronger than the other, or stronger than what happens, nothing would happen. There has to be weakness....

—*Jacques Derrida (2001, p. 64)*

Contents

Acknowledgments

When my book *Beyond Learning: Democratic Education for a Human Future* was published in 2006 it felt like the end of a long journey. *Beyond Learning* contained ideas I had been working on since the late 1990s and was a first attempt to bring them together in a book-length publication. Doing so was first of all helpful for me, as it allowed me to see themes and connections I had not really appreciated before. This is why I suggested, carefully, that the ideas in the book perhaps amounted to a theory of education. Others recognized this too, as became clear in the responses from reviewers, colleagues, students, and, perhaps most notably, from teachers and teacher educators working in a wide range of different contexts and settings around the world. The ideas in the book apparently struck a chord with them. Readers came to appreciate the versatility of the idea of a "pedagogy of interruption" and the joint concepts of "coming into the world" and "uniqueness" with which I aimed to articulate an educational vocabulary that would make it possible to respond to the challenge of thinking and "doing" education without the possession of a truth about what the human subject is or should become. Readers also responded positively to my attempt to explore a more intrinsic connection between education and democracy and to my critique of the impact of a "new language of learning" on education.

In the book that followed in 2010, *Good Education in an Age of Measurement,* I added several things to the discussion. Perhaps the most significant one was the introduction of a framework that allowed me to locate the ideas developed in *Beyond Learning* within a wider discussion about the functions and purposes of education. In *Good Education* I suggested that educational processes and practices always operate in three overlapping domains to which I referred as *qualification, socialization,* and *subjectification.* On the one hand the distinction between these domains allowed me to argue that questions about good education always need to be addressed in relation to what one aims to achieve—there is never anything good or desirable about educational processes and practices themselves—also highlighting that education is never one-dimensional in its intentions and ambitions so that there is always the difficult question of how to strike the right balance. On the other hand the framework allowed me to show with more clarity that the main focus of *Beyond Learning* had been on the subjectification dimension of education, that is, on the ways in which education contributes to the ways in which "newcomers" come into the world as unique, singular beings—to put it in the language of *Beyond Learning*. I could thus make clear that subjectification is not the be-all and end-all of education, although I would maintain that without an interest in this dimension education runs the risk of becoming just another instrument of social reproduction. The chapters in *Good Education* were then partly meant to explain why the question of purpose, the question as to what education is *for,* had almost disappeared from the educational discussion—something that I connected to debates about evidence and accountability in education and the wider "learnification" of educational discourses—and partly to provide those who share my concern for good education in the broad sense of the word with a language to (re)engage with questions of purpose in a more explicit and more deliberate manner. This I did by further developing the notion of a "pedagogy of interruption," the question of democratic education, and the idea of educational inclusion.

The present book in a sense concludes the trajectory I began in *Beyond Learning*. It focuses on a theme that was implicit in the other two books but that, in my view, deserves a more explicit treatment, not in the least because it has important implications for the ways in which one might wish to engage with my ideas in practical settings such as schools, colleges, and universities, or in relation to adult or community education. The aim of the present book is to explore different dimensions of what I will refer to as the *weakness* of education. The weakness of education refers to the fact that educational processes and practices do not work in a machine-like way. The argument I put forward in this book is that the weakness of education should *not* be seen as a problem that needs to be overcome, but should rather be understood as the very "dimension" that makes educational processes and practices *educational.* This is why any attempt to eradicate the weakness of education, any attempt to make education into a perfectly operating machine—something that is not entirely impossible, although I will argue that the price to pay for this is in most if not all cases too high—ultimately turns education against itself. The weakness of education thus signals that any engagement in education—both by educators and by those being educated—always entails a *risk.* The main premise of this book is that we should embrace this risk and see it as something positive that properly belongs to all education worthy of the name.

Although I did not set out to write a trilogy when I was working on the manuscript of *Beyond Learning,* the three books I eventually wrote do hang together to such an extent that I would now say, with more confidence, that together they constitute a theory of education. (The Appendix at the end of this book contains an interview that was conducted in 2011. It provides a brief overview of the key ideas of this theory of education.) The ideas in these books are, however, no more than "beginnings" in the Arendtian sense of the word. For them to become real they need to be taken up by others in ways that are necessarily beyond my control and my intentions. For them to become real, in other words, they need to be "risked." In this sense what is presented in this and the two preceding books should first and foremost be seen as an invitation for further theoretical and practical work. I am less concerned about the extent to which such work will stick to the letter of what I have written, but I do hope that it will be conducted in a similar spirit.

Writing this book has been an interesting experience. The process has been more difficult than I anticipated it to be and has also been more difficult than my previous writing projects. While I had the ambition to create a book with strong unity and consistency and a strong "logic," I realized, while writing, that the material I was working with—the ideas, the texts, the phrases, and the language—not always allowed me to go where I wanted to go. In this respect the creation of this book taught me the very lesson that this book is about: that any act of creation (including education) is at best a dialogue between one's intentions and the material one works with, and thus a process in which both have a voice and both have a role to play. The "logic" of the argument presented in this book is therefore, as I put it in the Prologue, more kaleidoscopic than linear. It provides a range of perspectives on the main themes of the book rather than proceeding as one unfolding line of argument. I nevertheless hope that what I have brought together in the pages that follow will provide some useful "beginnings."

I had the opportunity to experiment with the ideas in this book in a number of different contexts and settings. I would like to thank Herner Saeverot for the opportunity to give the overall argument of this book a first "try out," and for his encouragement to articulate the existential thrust of my ideas more explicitly. I would also like to acknowledge the work of John D. Caputo as a source of inspiration and encouragement for advancing the argument about the weakness of education. He also provided inspiration for the title of this book. The work I did with Denise Egéa-Kuehne on Derrida and education has had a lasting impact on my thinking. I am also grateful for the opportunity she provided to reflect on Levinas and pedagogy. I wish to thank Jim Garrison for our conversations about pragmatism, including the ones that helped me to see some of its limits and limitations, and Sam Rocha for important feedback on my reflections on teaching and transcendence. Working with Charles Bingham has substantially deepened my understanding of the educational significance of the work of Jacques Rancière, particularly in relation to questions about emancipation. Chris Higgins provided me with an opportunity to explore the work of Hannah Arendt in more depth. I would like to thank him, Wouter Pols, and Joop Berding for comments that helped me to deepen my ideas about education and political existence. Wouter Pols, Carlo Willman, and Janet Orchard provided opportunities for developing my ideas about teaching and teacher education. Many of the ideas in this book were also discussed with students and colleagues at the University of Stirling and at Örebro University and Mälardalen University. Tomas Englund has been a wonderful host during my visiting professorship at Örebro University, while Carl Anders Säfström has provided me with a very stimulating environment during my visiting professorship at Mälardalen University. Finally, I would like to thank Jason Barry and Dean Birkenkamp at Paradigm Publishers for their confidence in this project and for their ongoing support.

I dedicate this book to those who have taught me.

On the Weakness of Education

This book is about what many teachers know but are increasingly being prevented from talking about: that education always involves a *risk*. The risk is not that teachers might fail because they are not sufficiently qualified. The risk is not that education might fail because it is not sufficiently based on scientific evidence. The risk is not that students might fail because they are not working hard enough or are lacking motivation. The risk is there because, as W. B. Yeats has put it, education is not about filling a bucket but about lighting a fire. The risk is there because education is not an interaction between robots but an encounter between human beings. The risk is there because students are not to be seen as objects to be molded and disciplined, but as subjects of action and responsibility. Yes, we do educate because we want results and because we want our students to learn and achieve. But that does not mean that an educational technology, that is, a situation in which there is a perfect match between "input" and "output," is either possible or desirable. And the reason for this lies in the simple fact that if we take the risk out of education, there is a real chance that we take out education altogether.

Yet taking the risk out of education is exactly what teachers are increasingly being asked to do. It is what policy makers, politicians, the popular press, "the public," and organizations such as the Organisation for Economic Co-operation and Development (OECD) and the World Bank increasingly seem to be expecting if not demanding from education. They want education to be strong, secure, and predictable, and want it to be risk-free at all levels. This is why the task of schooling is more and more being constructed as the

1

effective production of pre-defined "learning outcomes" in a small number of subjects or with regard to a limited set of identities such as that of the good citizen or the effective lifelong learner. It is also why there is a more general push for making education into a safe and risk-free space (see Stengel and Weems 2010). What should have been a matter of degree—the question, after all, is not whether education should achieve something or not, or whether educational spaces should be safe or not, but *what* education should achieve and to what extent this can be pre-specified, and *what kind* of safety is desirable and at which point the desire for safety becomes uneducational—has turned into an "either-or" situation in which the opportunity for teachers to exercise judgment has virtually disappeared.

The risk aversion that pervades contemporary education puts teachers in a very difficult position. While policy makers and politicians look at education in the abstract and from a distance and mainly see it through statistics and performance data that can easily be manipulated and about which one can easily have an opinion, teachers engage with real human beings and realize at once that education cannot be "fixed" that simply—or that it can only be "fixed" at a very high price. The desire to make education strong, secure, predictable, and risk-free is in a sense an attempt to wish this reality away. It is an attempt to deny that education always deals with living "material," that is, with human subjects, not with inanimate objects. The desire to make education strong, secure, predictable, and risk-free is an attempt to forget that at the end of the day education should aim at making itself dispensable—no teacher wants their students to remain eternal students—which means that education *necessarily* needs to have an orientation toward the freedom and independence of those being educated.

Surely, it is possible to make education work; it is possible to reduce the complexity and openness of human learning—and one could even say that the educational practices and institutions that have been developed over the centuries do precisely that (see Biesta 2010a). But such complexity reduction always comes at a price, and the moral, political, and educational question is, What price are we willing to pay for making education "work"? This is partly a pragmatic question, as it has to be addressed in relation to the question, What do we want education to work *for*? (see Biesta 2010b). But it always also involves careful judgment about the point where complexity reduction turns into unjustifiable and uneducational suppression and where suppression turns into oppression. To simply demand that education become strong, secure, predictable, and risk-free, and to see any deviation from this path as a problem that needs to be "solved," therefore misses the educational point in a number of ways.

One has to do with the *attitude* expressed in the desire to make education strong, secure, predictable, and risk-free. The French educationalist Philippe Meirieu has characterized this attitude as *infantile* (see Meirieu 2008, p. 12). He argues that to think that education can be put under total control denies the fact that the world is not simply at our disposal. It denies the fact that other human beings have their own ways of being and thinking, their own reasons and motivations that may well be very different from ours. To wish all this away is a denial of the fact that what and who are other to us are precisely that: *other*. It thus exemplifies a form of magical thinking in which the world only exists as a projection of our own mind and our own desires. Education is precisely concerned with the overcoming of this "original egocentrism," *not* by overriding or eradicating where the child or student is coming from but by establishing opportunities for *dialogue* with what or who is other (see ibid., p. 13). And a dialogue, unlike a contest, is not about winning and losing but about ways of relating in which justice can be done to all who take part.

To demand that education become strong, secure, predictable, and risk-free also misses the educational point in that it seems to assume that there are only two options available for education: either to give in to the desires of the child or to subject the child to the desires of society; either total freedom or total control. Yet the educational concern is not about taking sides with any of these options—which reflect the age-old opposition between educational progressivism and educational conservatism—or about finding a happy medium or compromise between the two. The educational concern rather lies in the *transformation of what is desired into what is desirable* (see Biesta 2010b). It lies in the transformation of what is *de facto* desired into what can *justifiably* be desired—a transformation that can never be driven from the perspective of the self and its desires, but always requires engagement with what or who is other (which makes the educational question also a question about democracy; see Biesta 2011b). It is therefore, again, a dialogical process. This makes the educational way the slow way, the difficult way, the frustrating way, and, so we might say, the weak way, as the outcome of this process can neither be guaranteed nor secured.

Yet we live in impatient times in which we constantly get the message that instant gratification of our desires is possible and that it is good. The call to make education strong, secure, predictable, and risk-free is an expression of this impatience. But it is based on a fundamental misunderstanding of what education is about and a fundamental misunderstanding of what makes education "work." It sees the weakness of education—the fact that there will never be a perfect match between educational "input" and "output"—*only* as a defect, *only* as something that needs to be addressed and overcome, and not *also* as the very condition that makes education possible (see also Vanderstraeten and Biesta 2006). It is this misguided impatience that pushes education into a direction where teachers' salaries and even their jobs are made dependent upon their alleged ability to increase their students' exam scores. It is this misguided impatience that has resulted in the medicalization of education, where children are being made fit for the educational system, rather than that we ask where the causes of this misfit lie and who, therefore, needs treatment most: the child or society. The educational way, the slow, difficult, frustrating, and weak way, may therefore not be the most popular way in an impatient society. But in the long run it may well turn out to be the only *sustainable* way, since we all know that systems aimed at the total control of what human beings do and think eventually collapse under their own weight, if they have not already been cracked open from the inside before.

The chapters in this book, therefore, come to education from the angle of its weakness. In them I try to show how, for what reasons, and under what circumstances the weakness of education—the acknowledgment that education isn't a mechanism and shouldn't be turned into one—matters. This book is not an unbridled celebration of all things weak, but an attempt to show, on the one hand, that education only works through weak connections of communication and interpretation, of interruption and response, and, on the other hand, that this weakness matters if our educational endeavors are informed by a concern for those we educate to be subjects of their own actions—which is as much about being the author and originator of one's actions as it is about being responsible for what one's actions bring about.

Such an orientation toward the child or student as a subject in its own right is, of course, not all that matters in education. As I have argued elsewhere in more detail (see Biesta 2010b), there are (at least) three domains in which education can function and thus three domains in which educational purposes can be articulated. One is the domain of *qualification,* which has to do with the acquisition of knowledge, skills, values, and dispositions. The second is the domain of *socialization,* which has to do with the ways in which, through education, we become part of existing traditions and ways of doing and being. The third is the domain of *subjectification,* which has to do with the interest of education in the subjectivity or "subject-ness" of those we educate. It has to do with emancipation and freedom and with the responsibility that comes with such freedom. The weakness of education is at stake in all three dimensions, but how much we value this weakness depends crucially on the extent to which we believe that education is not just about the reproduction of what we already know or of what already exists, but is genuinely interested in the ways in which new beginnings and new beginners can come into the world (see Biesta 2006a; Winter 2011). Such an orientation, therefore, is not just about how we can get the world into our children and students; it is also—and perhaps first of all—about how we can help our children and students to engage with, and thus come into, the world.

In the seven chapters that follow I explore the weakness of educational processes and practices from a range of different angles and in relation to a number of key educational themes. The themes I have chosen are creativity, communication, teaching, learning, emancipation, democracy, and virtuosity. I start, in Chapter 1, with the theme of *creativity*. While much work on creativity focuses on the ways in which education might foster the creativity of students, I approach the question of educational creativity from a different angle. On the one hand I am interested in education as itself a creative process—that is, as a process that creates; on the other hand I am interested in how we might best understand what it means to create, and more specifically, what it means to see education as a process that in some way contributes to the creation of human subjectivity. Taking inspiration from the work of John Caputo, I make a distinction between two understandings of creation: strong metaphysical creation and weak existential creation. While the first has had a dominant influence on Western ideas about what it means to create—both in secular and in religious discourses—Caputo shows, through a reading of the creation stories in the book of Genesis, that the act of creation can be—and in a sense ought to be—understood outside of the domain of omnipotence, strength, and metaphysics. It is the weak understanding of creation that I bring to bear on the question of human subjectivity through an engagement with the work of Emmanuel Levinas. Here subjectivity is not understood as an essence but as an event, and thus as something that can only be captured in existential and, therefore, weak terms. Doing so allows me to show how the weakness of education matters for what, to me, indeed lies at the heart of any educational endeavor, which is the emergence of human subjectivity.

As education is at heart a dialogical process, I focus, in Chapter 2, on the theme of *communication*. In the first part of the chapter I discuss how communication has been understood and theorized in the work of John Dewey, both at a general level and with regard to educational processes and practices. Unlike the sender-receiver model that still seems to inform much commonsense thinking about communication—in education and elsewhere—Dewey provides a conception of communication as a meaning-generating process where things are literally made "in common" through interaction and participation. Such an understanding of communication-as-participation has important implications for education, both at the micro-level of the communication of meaning in classrooms and schools and at the macro-level of the interaction between cultures and traditions or, with a more general phrase, the interaction "across difference." But it is precisely here that there is a problem with Dewey's philosophy of communication, and to indicate what the problem is, I turn to the work of Jacques Derrida. With Derrida I argue that Dewey's shift from a consciousness-centered philosophy to a communication-centered philosophy still tries to "frame" communication and in this sense runs the risk of not being able to take its own communicative intent entirely seriously. That is why I argue that in order for this philosophy of communication to do educational and political "work" it needs to risk itself *in* communication—a gesture to which I refer as *deconstructive* (not deconstructed) pragmatism.

The idea that education is at heart a dialogical process, further amplified by ideas of communication as interaction and participation, might give the impression that I am advocating an understanding of education as a process in which people learn together through interaction and dialogue. This has indeed become a popular and even fashionable idea in contemporary educational discourse and practice, as can be seen in such notions as "communities of practice" and "learning communities." But to think of education in these terms runs the risk of eradicating what I see as essential for education, which is the presence of a teacher, not just as a fellow learner or a facilitator of learning, but as someone who, in the most general terms, has to bring something to the educational situation that was not there already. In Chapter 3 I therefore engage with the theme of *teaching,* arguing that in order to understand what teaching is "about," we need to connect it to an idea of "transcendence"—teaching as something that radically comes from the "outside." I stage the discussion of teaching and transcendence partly in relation to the rise of constructivism in education and partly in relation to a "maieutic" understanding of teaching, that is, of teaching as an act of midwifery, and show how along both lines there is a risk of eradicating the teacher from (our understanding of) the educational process. There is, however, a caveat in that the "power" to teach should not be understood as a power that is in the possession of the teacher. Through a discussion of the distinction between "learning from" and "being taught by" I highlight the fact that the gift of teaching is in a sense an impossible gift—a gift that can be received, but not a gift that in a positive or strong sense can be given by the teacher.

In Chapter 4 I turn to the theme of *learning.* Against the idea that learning is some kind of natural phenomenon that is simply available for theorizing, research, and educational intervention, I argue that learning is something constructed—that when we refer to something as "learning" we are not engaged in a description of a naturally occurring phenomenon but are actually making a judgment about change. Such judgments are important in educational settings, but it is important to see them for what they are, that is, normative judgments about desirable change, not descriptions of inevitable natural processes. To see learning as something constructed and artificial makes it possible to expose the political "work" done through the idea of "learning," something that I discuss in terms of the "politics of learning." Against the background of an analysis of the politics of learning that is at work in contemporary discussions about lifelong learning, I show how the idea of learning as something natural runs the risk of keeping people in their place. This is why in the later parts of the chapter I turn to the theme of emancipation in order to explore whether it is possible to think of emancipation outside of the confines of a certain politics of learning. With Foucault I explore the emancipatory potential of the ideas of resistance, interruption, and transgression in order to highlight the need for resisting the idea of the learner identity as a natural and inevitable identity and for interrupting the current "common sense" about learning.

From these more fundamental questions about teaching and learning I turn, in Chapter 5, to what is perhaps one of the most difficult educational questions, namely, the question whether, and if so how, education can contribute to the freedom of the human subject. This is the theme of *emancipation*. I discuss aspects of the philosophical and educational history of the concept of emancipation in order to highlight a common thread in the modern understanding of emancipation where emancipation is seen as a "powerful intervention" from the outside in order to set someone free. In the chapter I not only raise a number of questions about this particular understanding of emancipation—questions that reveal an underlying "colonial" way of thinking in the modern "logic" of emancipation—but also outline a different understanding of emancipation. In this conception, which is informed by the work of Jacques Rancière, equality is not seen as an "end-state" to be achieved at some moment in the future, but rather functions as an assumption that requires verification; that is, it requires to be "made true" through our actions in the here and now. Such an understanding of emancipation is no longer based on (the possibility of) a "powerful intervention" from the outside but rather occurs in events of subjectification, when individuals resist existing identities and identity-positions and speak on their own terms.

The question of emancipation so conceived is not only an educational question but is at the very same time a political question. That is why, in Chapter 6, I connect it to the theme of *democracy*. My discussion partner in this chapter is Hannah Arendt. Arendt's work poses a real challenge to anyone who is interested in the relationships between education and democracy, as she has been one of the most outspoken critics of the idea that education and politics may have anything to do with each other. She takes the view that the realm of education should be "divorced" from all other realms, and most of all from the realm of political life. In the chapter I show that Arendt's arguments for this position are based on a psychological understanding of education, one that assumes that the only available vocabulary for education is that of development, preparation, identity, and control, so that notions like action, plurality, subjectivity, and freedom only begin to matter once children have gone through a particular developmental trajectory that makes them "ready" for democratic politics. Using some of Arendt's own arguments, I show that once we overcome such a psychological view of education it becomes possible to reveal the intimate connection between education and democratic politics. Using Arendt's understanding of freedom as "being-together-in-plurality" I argue that such freedom cannot be "produced" educationally but can only be achieved politically. This provides the starting point for an understanding of democratic education that is neither psychological nor moral, but rather thoroughly educational.

In Chapter 7, the final chapter of the book, I return to teaching and the teacher through a discussion of the theme of *virtuosity*. Against the idea of teaching as a science-based or evidence-based profession, but also against the idea of teaching as a matter of competence and competencies, I develop the idea of teaching as virtue based. Against the background of a critical analysis of recent policy and theory around teacher education I raise the question whether teaching should be understood as an art or a science. After briefly considering the problems with the idea of education as a science with the help of William James, I turn to Aristotle's distinction between *poiesis* ("making action") and *praxis* ("doing action") in order to argue that the more important question is not *whether* teaching is an art or a science, but *what kind of an art* teaching actually is. While to some extent and in some respect there may well be a production dimension to teaching, I argue that teaching is never exhausted by the idea of production—not in the least because as teachers we never produce our students; they are always already there as human subjects in their own right. The educational question is therefore never just about *how* to do things, but always involves judgments about *what is to be done*—the question of educational desirability—and this locates education firmly within the domain of *praxis*. The distinction between *poiesis* and *praxis* helps us to see that teachers do not just need knowledge about how to do things (*techne*) but also, and most of all, need practical wisdom (*phronesis*) in order to judge what needs to be done. Teachers therefore need not simply to be competent, but also to be educationally wise. Such wisdom is to be understood as a "quality" of the person. Aristotle calls this quality *arete* (αρετή), which can be translated as "character"—in the sense of a way of being and acting that characterizes the person—or also as "virtue." With a play on the latter word I then suggest that teachers need educational virtuosity: the ability to make situated judgments about what is educationally desirable.

In the Epilogue I bring the main threads of the book together in an argument for a pedagogy of the event, a pedagogy that favors existence over essence, weakness over strength, *praxis* over *poiesis,* and thus a pedagogy that is willing to engage with the beautiful risk inherent in all education worthy of the name.

CHAPTER ONE

Creativity

In the beginning God created the heaven and the earth.

In recent years there has been a flurry of publications and reports about the role of creativity in education. The general tenor of this work is that creativity is a good thing that deserves to be promoted in schools, colleges, and universities, particularly as an antidote to those forms of education that are considered to "stifle" creativity. The emphasis in these discussions is, however, almost entirely on the creativity of children and young people. In this chapter I approach the question of creativity from a different angle. I am interested in education as itself a creative "act" or, to be more precise, in education as an act of creation, that is, as an act of bringing something new into the world, something that did not exist before. I am particularly interested in seeing education as a process that in some way contributes to the creation of human subjectivity—and I will qualify below why I think that it is appropriate to think of education in these terms.

To think of education as an act of creation leads us straight into the major theme of this book, which is whether we can only think of creation in strong terms, that is, as the *production* of something—literally the production of some *thing*; or whether it is possible and desirable to think of the act of creation in a different—that is, a weak—way. While "creativity" is a relatively noncontentious notion that seems to have a "feel good" factor about it—harking back to romantic notions of the child as a naturally creative being—the notion of "creation" is far more contentious. This partly has to do with the central role creation narratives play in almost all cultures (see Leeming 2010) and partly with the predominant interpretation of the creation narrative in the book of Genesis. In this interpretation creation is depicted as a powerful act by means of which God has brought reality into existence.

This particular interpretation has haunted both secular and religious discourses up to the present day. It has led to an opposition between those who base their religious beliefs on the idea of this powerful divine act of creation out of nothingness—*creatio ex nihilo*—and those who reject such creationism in favor of a scientific explanation of the origins of the universe. The irony, however, is that both parties are in a sense after the same thing, that is, the identification of a first original event from which everything else has emanated. God's act of creation out of nothingness is in this regard structurally similar to the idea of the Big Bang or the search for the most fundamental particle—sometimes called the "God particle"—from which the universe is made. The problem with such strategies is that by trying to identify an origin, they always raise the question of the origin of the origin, the question of what came before. As long as we think of creation in causal terms, we end up either with an infinite regress or with an arbitrary stop—something Aristotle realized when he posited the idea of the "unmoved mover" as the first cause of the world of motion.

The question I ask in this chapter is whether it is possible to think of creation differently, that is, not in strong metaphysical terms—in terms of causes and effects—but in weak existential terms—in terms of encounters and events. I develop my answer to this question in two steps. In the first part of the chapter I follow John D. Caputo's deconstructive reading of the book of Genesis in order to show that the predominant understanding of the "act" of creation is not the whole story and that an entirely different understanding of what creation entails is actually available—one in which risk plays a central role. In the second part of the chapter I connect this to the question of the educational interest in human subjectivity. Here I turn to the writings of Emmanuel Levinas and his "ethics of subjectivity" in order to suggest that human subjectivity should not be understood in natural terms, that is, as part of our essence, but rather in existential terms, that is, as a "quality" of our relationships with what or who is other. Subjectivity is, in other words, not something we can have or possess, but something that can be realized, from time to time, in always new, open, and unpredictable situations of encounter. Understanding subjectivity as an ethical event leaves us, in a sense, empty-handed as educators. Yet I will argue that it is precisely the experience of empty-handedness that can help us to understand what a weak understanding of the role of education in the event of subjectivity might entail.

THE BEAUTIFUL RISK OF CREATION

In his book *The Weakness of God,* John Caputo (2006) not only provides a different understanding of the "process" of creation but also argues that the way in which creation has commonly been understood, that is, as the act of an omnipotent God, is actually a Hellenistic invention. As Caputo explains, the God "whose act was to be cleaned up by metaphysics and made into pure act ... was God blended from biblical poetry and Platonic and Aristotelian metaphysics" (ibid., p. 73; see also p. 59). This is the God who, in the King James translation, was there "in the beginning" and from that position "created the heaven and the earth" (Genesis 1:1, King James Version). This formulation, as Caputo puts it, expresses "sheer, clean, lean, perfect, stunning, uninhibited power" (2006, p. 56). But the Hellenistic reading of the opening sentence of the book of Genesis is quite different from a translation of the Hebrew text that has *not* gone through Greek metaphysics and that is *not* trying to depict God as the original origin, as the Aristotelian "unmoved mover."

In the King James Version we read, "In the beginning God created the heaven and the earth. And the earth was without form, and void; and darkness was upon the face of the deep. And the Spirit of God moved upon the face of the waters" (Genesis 1:1–2, King James Version). Yet in an alternative translation we get, "When God began creation, the earth was unformed and void, darkness was over the surface of the deep, and God's wind swept over the water."[1] The difference between this rendition and the previous one—and this small difference is absolutely crucial—is that in the latter translation when God began to create, "things had already begun" (Caputo 2006, p. 57). God (Elohim[2]) begins, as Caputo explains, "where he finds himself with co-everlasting but mute companions: a barren earth, lifeless waters, and a sweeping wind" (ibid., p. 57). What is God (Elohim) doing there? Caputo argues that God is not bringing earth (*tohu wa-bohu*), water (*tehom*), and wind (*ruach*) into being, but that he is rather *calling them into life* (see ibid., p. 58). The "astonishing thing" here is *not* that God creates something out of nothing but "that God *brings being into life*" (ibid., p. 58; emphasis in original). "That is the wonder," Caputo writes, "and that life that God breathes in them

---

1. Taken from http://en.wikipedia.org/wiki/Bereishit_(parsha) (accessed December 29, 2011). See also Caputo (2006), p. 57.

2. In the book of Genesis there are two names for "God": Elohim and YHWH (Yahweh). The latter is sometimes translated as "Lord" or as the "Lord God" in the King James Version.

is what God calls 'good,' which goes a step beyond being" (ibid., p. 58). God, therefore, is not "the power supply for everything that happens" but is "the source of good and its warrant" (ibid., p. 73).

There is, however, a second creation narrative in the book of Genesis, which is the story of Adam and Eve in the Garden of Eden. Here the protagonist is not Elohim but YHWH or Yahweh. The dominant mark of the first creation narrative, that of Elohim, is that of what Caputo, quoting Milan Kundera, calls "our 'categorical agreement with being'" (ibid., p. 66). The "rhythmic refrain" of this narrative is that of an "originary benediction, 'And God saw that it was good'" (ibid.). Caputo explains that in this narrative "Elohim creates by the word of his mouth" (ibid.). This means that Elohim "is not responsible for the fact that the elements are *there* but for the fact that they are fashioned and *called good*" (ibid., pp. 66–67; emphasis in original). It also means that creation is "not a movement from non-being to being, but from being to the good" (ibid., p. 67). But when YHWH, the Lord God, comes unto the scene,[3] we get a different verdict. No longer "good," not "evil" but, as Caputo argues, "guilty" (see ibid.).

Caputo describes the difference as follows: "If Elohim is a calm, distant, celestial, hands-off creator, Yahweh is very nervous about what he is getting himself into and is much more of a hands-on micro-manager" (ibid., p. 67). The crucial point for Caputo is that Yahweh, unlike Elohim, seems to have "little taste *for the risk of creation, for the risk of parenting*" (ibid., p. 68; emphasis in original)—a risk that Caputo, with reference to Levinas, refers to as "the beautiful risk of creation" (ibid., p. 60). Yahweh does not so much give Adam and Eve life as he gives them a *test* of life. "He gives them life on a kind of conditional trial loan to see if they are going to abuse it and try to become like him, in which case he is prepared to withdraw from the deal and wipe—or wash—them out" (ibid.); this is unlike the story of Elohim where life is what Derrida (1992a) would refer to as an *unconditional* gift. Yahweh, as Caputo puts it, "seems to have a bit of a short fuse, seems inordinately suspicious of his own creation, and is far too nervous about his offspring for a good parent" (ibid., p. 69).

There are two important observations here—observations that also have relevance for the discussion about education that is to follow. The first

---

3. It is important to note that historically the story of YHWH is thought to be of an earlier date than the story of Elohim. This is why it is significant that the author—or Redactor, as the author is called in the literature—of this part of Genesis has put the story of Elohim first. "First the good news, the Redactor seems to think, then the bad news" (Caputo 2006, p. 67).

point Caputo makes is that creating, "like procreating, is risky business, and one has to be prepared for a lot of noise, dissent, resistance, and a general disturbance of the peace if one is of a mind to engage in either" (ibid., p. 69). While Elohim appears to be willing to take this risk—knowing that real trust is always without ground, that it cannot be "returned," so to speak, that it is unconditional (see Biesta 2006a, chapter 1)—Yahweh remains *dis*trustful of his creation, appears to be unable to take the risk, or is only able to take the risk as a *conditional* risk. "Right from the start," Caputo writes, "Yahweh is hedging his bet" (ibid., p. 71).

The second observation is perhaps even more important for our discussion, as Caputo points out that whereas Elohim creates adult beings like himself, Yahweh wants to bring forth "eternal children" (ibid., p. 70). "Elohim wants images who are not children but adults, not faint images but robust ones, not bad copies but true ones" (ibid., pp. 70–71). Yahweh, in contrast, "has little heart for the risk that any parent takes, which is that their offspring will outstrip their intention and spin out of control, and things will not turn out as the parents planned" (ibid., p. 71). Yahweh prefers his creatures to remain children—seen but not heard. Right from the start Yahweh is therefore trying to "minimize the risk he is taking, and he has no tolerance for failure" (ibid., p. 71). This is why the original setting of his creation is not a "garden of delight" but rather "a minefield of tricks, traps, tests, trials, and temptation" (ibid., p. 71) where it is almost inevitable that his creatures will fail.

WEAKNESS, CREATION, AND THE GOOD

Caputo argues that we shouldn't think of the two creation stories as opposing accounts, as two options we have to choose from. He emphasizes that the Redactor who put these stories together in one narrative is making a bigger point. In the first narrative we find "the original covenant that Elohim makes with creation, which is that what he has made is good" (ibid., p. 71), whereas in the second narrative "that judgment is put to the test by showing us to what extent things go wrong" (ibid.). Neither creation narrative, however, sees creation as a transition from nothingness into something. "These stories tell, not of an omnipotent creator creating *ex nihilo*, which stretches our credulity, but of a maker making something over which he has only so much control and no more" (ibid., p. 71).

Here lies the significance of the elements God has to work with. These elements—earth (*tohu wa-bohu*), water (*tehom*), and wind (*ruach*)—"are not evil, just fluid; they are not wicked, just unwieldy; they are not demonic, just determinable, flexible and unprogrammable" (ibid., p. 72). There is therefore an element in them "which is not precisely God's image but in which God is trying to fashion his image, a certain irreducible alterity that God wants to cultivate, fertilize, plant, order, and bring round to the divine way of doing things but whose irreducibility and resistance the Lord God is just going to have to learn to live with and hope for the best" (ibid.). The elements thus signify "a certain limit on God's power and call for God's patience" (ibid.). God, "like any good parent, must learn to deal with the unpredictability and the unforeseeability, the foolishness, and even the destructiveness of his children, in the hope that they will grow up and eventually come around" (ibid.). What makes the two creation stories different is not their account of creation but the different *attitudes* Elohim and Yahweh take to creation. Caputo summarizes the difference as follows: "Elohim is cool; Yahweh is a nervous wreck" (ibid.).

What we are getting through these creation stories is the announcement of "a kind of covenant with life that we are asked to initial" (ibid., p. 74). As Caputo explains, "We are asked to say 'yes' to life by adding a second yes to God's 'yes' (Rosenzweig); to countersign God's yes with our yes, and that involves signing on to that risk; to embrace what God has formed and the elemental undecidability in which God has formed or inscribed it" (ibid., p. 74). Caputo adds that God "indeed has a plan for creation, but God, like the rest of us, is hoping it works" (ibid.)—and this hope is, in the end, all there is. Against this background Caputo refers to Walter Benjamin's contention that history is "one single catastrophe which keeps piling wreckage upon wreckage" and that we are driven through time by "a storm blowing from Paradise" (ibid., p. 74). Caputo contends that Benjamin "was right enough," as in the very next chapter "Cain murders Abel and the bloody course of history is launched" (ibid.). But this is not the only wind blowing out of Paradise. There is "a gentler breeze that pronounces all things 'good'" (ibid., p. 75). This other gesture of creation "gives the world significance, not a cause, a meaning, not a metaphysical explanation" (ibid., p. 75). By placing this narrative first the Redactor of Genesis is saying that "for all of its violence and ferocity, we cannot let the storm of the catastrophe, the history of ruins, overwhelm us" (ibid.).

So where does that leave God? It basically leaves God without power. Or to be more precise: it leaves God without metaphysical power, without causal power, without omnipotent power, without Hellenistic power, so to speak. According to Caputo—and I agree—this is not a bad thing. To think of God as omnipotent in the metaphysical sense of the word is actually a dangerous fantasy as "the sovereignty of God is readily extended to the sovereignty of man over other man, over women and animals, over all creation" (ibid., p. 79)—which is why he writes that omnipotence is not a mystery but actually "a mystification and a conceptual mistake" (ibid.). "The very idea of 'creation from nothing' and of divine 'omnipotence' has the fundamental mark of idealizing, epistemological and psychoanalytic fantasy, that is, the removal of all limits imposed by reality, carrying out an action in an ideal space where there is absolute perfect control and no trace of resistance from the real" (ibid., pp. 79–80). It is, as I have put it in the Prologue, an *infantile* attitude, not a grown-up one. Against the idea of God as a strong force and of creation as an act of bringing being into existence, Caputo thus presents "the event that stirs in the name of God" as a "weak force" (ibid., p. 84) and helps us to see creation as a confirmation of what is already there as "beautiful and *good*" (ibid., p. 86). The event of creation is thus that of bringing being to life by affirming its goodness. That is all there is to creation. And it is a very risky business, not a matter of omnipotence. We might even say that engaging in the business of creation in this way expresses a belief. But not belief in the cognitive sense, not belief in a set of propositions as in "I believe this, this, and that," but a belief in life, in the goodness of life, and in goodness itself.

Along these lines Caputo thus helps us to see that the "choice"—if that is the right word—is not between creationism and anti-creationism, is not between creationism and its rejection. It rather is between what we might call "strong metaphysical creationism"—where creation is an act of unbridled power—and "weak existential creationism"—where creation is an event through which being is brought to life. The choice, so we might say, is therefore a choice between essence and existence, between metaphysics and life, between whether we want to take the risk of life—with all the uncertainty, unpredictability, and frustration that come with it—or whether we look for certainty outside, underneath, or beyond life. The quest for certainty, as John Dewey also knew, always gets us into trouble, not only because of the many conflicting certainties that are always on offer but also because this quest keeps us away from engaging with life itself—it keeps us away from the things that are right in front of our eyes, the things that really matter and that require our attention, right here and right now. Which brings me to the question of education.

THE SUBJECT OF EDUCATION

I have indicated in the Prologue that education functions in (at least) three areas: that of qualification, that of socialization, and that of what I have referred to as subjectification. While the question of what it means to create in and through education is relevant in all three domains, I wish to confine myself in this chapter to the dimension of subjectification, that is, to the way in which educational processes and practices contribute to the emergence of human subjectivity or "subject-ness." Subjectification, so we might say, expresses a particular interest—an interest in the subjectivity or subject-ness of those being educated—that is, in the assumption that those at whom our educational efforts are directed are not to be seen as objects but as subjects in their own right; subjects of action and responsibility. The interest in the subjectivity of those we educate is perhaps a modern interest, as it is connected to notions of freedom and independence that gained prominence in educational thought and practice from the Enlightenment onward (see Biesta 2006a). One could say that it is only from then on that it becomes possible and important to make a distinction between socialization—which is about the ways in which, through education, individuals become part of existing orders and traditions—and subjectification—which is about ways of being that are not entirely determined by existing orders and traditions.

By using the notions of subjectivity, subjectification, and subject-ness I am not advancing a particular conception of human subjectivity or a particular theory about how subjectivity "emerges." There are different answers to be given to these questions, and by identifying the subject-ness of those being educated as a proper educational interest I am trying to be open to the different ways in which subject-ness and its educational emergence might be understood. The notions of subjectivity and subjectification, to put it differently, do not in themselves articulate a particular conception or theory of subject-ness and its emergence. I am, however, avoiding certain other words and concepts, most notably the notion of *identity*—which for me has more to do with the ways in which we identify with existing orders and traditions than with ways of acting and being that are "outside" of this—and also the notion of *individuality*—which tends to depict the human subject too much in isolation from other human beings. By using the notion of *emergence* I am also, for the moment, trying to be open about the "how" of subjectification, although the word I am deliberately avoiding here is *development*, as I do not think that the emergence of subjectivity should be understood in developmental terms, not, that is, if development is located in the domain of being (see below). Although the notion of *subjectification* may have negative connotations as it hints at forms of subjection, I will argue that it is the "echo" of a certain kind of subjection that is actually very relevant for how I will propose to understand subjectivity and its emergence.

When I suggested in the introduction to this chapter that I was interested in seeing education as a process that in some way contributes to the creation of human subjectivity, this may have sounded preposterous. If we think of creation in the strong, metaphysical sense, then the idea that we as educators create our students doesn't make any sense at all. But with Caputo we not only have a different way to approach the whole idea of creation; his ideas also help us to ask whether human subjectivity can only be understood in terms of being, essence, and nature—that is, in strong metaphysical terms—or whether it is possible, and perhaps even desirable or necessary, to understand human subjectivity in weak existential terms. To explore this latter option I return to the work of Emmanuel Levinas—and I say "return" because Levinas continues to be a source of inspiration for my understanding of the question of human subjectivity (see Biesta 2006a, 2010b; Winter 2011), and his ideas on this matter are too important not to be mentioned in the context of this book.

AN ETHICS OF SUBJECTIVITY

The work of Emmanuel Levinas is uniquely concerned with the question of human subjectivity (see, e.g., Critchley 1999; Bauman 1993). Yet instead of offering us a new theory or truth about the human subject, Levinas has articulated a completely different "avenue" toward the question of human subjectivity, one in which an ethical category—responsibility—is singled out as "the essential, primary and fundamental structure of subjectivity" (Levinas 1985, p. 95). Levinas's thinking thus poses a challenge to the "wisdom of the Western tradition and Western thought" in which it is assumed that human beings "are human through consciousness" (Levinas 1998a, p. 190). He challenges the idea of the subject as a substantial center of meaning and initiative, as a *cogito* who is first of all concerned with itself and only then, perhaps, if he or she decides to be so, with the other. Levinas argues instead that the subject is always *already* engaged in a relationship that is "older than the ego, prior to principles" (Levinas 1981, p. 117). This relationship is neither a knowledge relationship nor a willful act of the ego. It is an *ethical* relationship, a relationship of infinite and unconditional responsibility for the Other.[4]

Levinas stresses that this responsibility for the Other is not a responsibility that we can choose to take upon us, as this would only be possible if we were an ego or a consciousness *before* we were "inscribed" in this relationship.

---

4. I follow the convention among translators of Levinas to use Other with a capital "O" as the translation of "autrui"—the personal other—as distinguished from "other" with a lowercase "o" as the translation of "autre"—otherness or alterity in general.

This responsibility, which is the "essential, primary and fundamental structure of subjectivity," is therefore a responsibility *"that is justified by no prior commitment"* (ibid., p. 102; emphasis in original). It is, as Levinas puts it, a "passion" that is absolute. This means, however, that the question of subjectivity is not about the *being* of the subject but about "my right to be" (Levinas 1989, p. 86). As Levinas argues, it is only in the "very crisis of the being of a being" (ibid., p. 85), in the *interruption* of its being, that the uniqueness (see below) of the subject first acquires meaning (see also Levinas 1981, p. 13). This interruption constitutes the relationship of responsibility, which is a responsibility of "being-in-question" (ibid., p. 111). It is this being-in-question, this "assignation to answer without evasions," that "assigns the self to be a self" and thus calls me as this unique individual (ibid., p. 106). This is why Levinas describes the "oneself," the unique individual, as the "not-being-able-to-slip-away-from an assignation," an assignation that does not aim at any generality but is aimed at *me* (ibid., p. 127). The oneself, therefore, "does not coincide with the identifying of truth, is not statable in terms of consciousness, discourse and intentionality" (ibid., p. 106). The oneself is a singularity "prior to the distinction between the particular and the universal," and therefore both unsayable and unjustifiable (ibid., p. 107). The oneself is not a being but is "beyond the normal play of action and passion in which the identity of a being is maintained, in which it *is*" (ibid., p. 114).

By identifying responsibility as the "essential, primary and fundamental structure of subjectivity," Levinas tries to get away from the idea that human subjectivity can be understood in essential terms, that is, as a metaphysical essence. Levinas acknowledges that he describes subjectivity in ethical terms, but he hastens to add that "ethics, here, does not supplement a preceding existential base" (Levinas 1985, p. 95). This is why I would like to suggest that Levinas does not provide us with a new *theory* of subjectivity—a theory that would claim, for example, that the subject is a being endowed with certain moral qualities, capacities, or response-abilities—but rather with an *ethics* of subjectivity (see also Biesta 2008). Levinas urges us to approach the "question" of subjectivity in ethical terms, that is, in terms of being made responsible and taking up one's responsibility. Levinas is therefore not trying to answer the question as to what the subject *is*—what its nature is, what its essence is—but rather is interested in how subjectivity *exists* or, to be more precise, how my "subject-ness" is possible, how it can appear or manifest itself. This is never a question of subjectivity in general—which is another reason why there is no theory of subjectivity in Levinas—but is a question of *my* unique subjectivity as it emerges from my singular, unique responsibility.

The question of uniqueness, however, is again not a question that can be answered by looking at the characteristics that make me different from everyone else. For Levinas uniqueness is not a matter of our essence or nature—which also means that it is not a matter of identity. When we use identity to articulate our uniqueness, we focus on the ways in which I am *different* from the other—which might be called *uniqueness-as-difference* (see also Biesta 2010b, chapter 4). In that case we make use of the other to articulate our own uniqueness. We might say, therefore, that identity is based upon an instrumental rather than an ethical relation with the other. The question for Levinas, however, is not about what *makes* each of us unique. Instead, he looks for situations *in which it matters* that I am unique, that is, situations in which I cannot be replaced or substituted by someone else. These are situations in which someone calls me, in which someone does an appeal to me, in which someone singles me out. These are not situations in which I *am* unique, but situations in which my uniqueness *matters*—where it matters that I am I and not someone else. These are situations in which I am *singularized*—situations where *uniqueness-as-irreplaceability* emerges—and thus situations where the event of subjectivity *happens.* Subjectivity-as-irreplaceability, subjectivity-as-responsibility, is therefore *not* a different or other way of being of the subject, because, as Levinas argues, "being otherwise is still being" (Levinas 1985, p. 100). The uniqueness of the subject and subjectivity-as-uniqueness rather emerge in a "domain" that lies "beyond essence," so to speak, a non-place or "null-site" as Levinas puts it (Levinas 1981, p. 8) that is *otherwise than being.*

The uniqueness of the human subject is thus to be understood as something that goes precisely against what Levinas calls the "ontological condition" of human beings. This is why he writes that to be human means "to live as if one were not a being among beings" (Levinas 1985, p. 100). Or as Lingis puts it, "The self cannot be conceived as an entity. It has dropped out of being" (Lingis 1981, p. xxxi). What makes me unique, what singles me out, what singularizes me, is the fact that my responsibility is not transferable. Levinas summarizes it as follows: "Responsibility is what is incumbent on me exclusively, and what, humanly, I cannot refuse. This charge is a supreme dignity of the unique. I am I in the sole measure that I am responsible, a non-interchangeable I. I can substitute myself for everyone, but no one can substitute himself for me" (Levinas 1985, p. 101). This is also why responsibility is not reciprocal. The Other may well be responsible for me, but Levinas emphasizes that this is totally the affair of the Other. The intersubjective relation is a nonsymmetrical relationship. "I am responsible for the Other without waiting for reciprocity, were I to die for it" (ibid., p. 98). It is precisely insofar as the relationship between the Other and me is *not* reciprocal that I am subjected to the Other, and it is in this way that my subjectivity becomes possible. In this sense we might say that my subjectivity is to be found in my subjection to the Other, which means, in the shortest formula, that for Levinas "the subject is subject" (Critchley 1999, p. 63).

A Pedagogy with Empty Hands

If we follow Levinas in his suggestion that uniqueness is not a matter of essence but of existence, that it is not a matter of being but of "otherwise than being," then it follows that subjectivity or subject-ness ceases to be an attribute of something (literally of some *thing*) and instead becomes an *event*: something that can *occur* from time to time, something that can emerge, rather than something that is constantly there, that we can have, possess, and secure. This is so because for Levinas subjectivity is not to be confused with responsibility. Our responsibility is simply "there," it is given; our subjectivity, in contrast, has to do with what we do with this responsibility, how we respond to it or, with a phrase from Zygmunt Bauman (1998): how we take responsibility for our responsibility. While my uniqueness matters in those situations in which I am "called" to responsibility, in those situations in which I cannot be replaced since it is *I* who is being called, not "the subject" in general, the question of whether I take up this responsibility and respond to the assignation is an entirely different matter. With regard to this, Levinas is adamant that I am only responsible for my own responsibility. What others do with their responsibility is entirely up to them. I cannot *make* anyone else responsible.

The latter point is of crucial importance for education, as we shouldn't make the mistake of thinking that now that Levinas has provided us with a new understanding of subjectivity, we can embark on a program of moral education so as to make our students into responsible human beings. This would immediately pull the event of subjectivity back into the domain of being and thus would miss the very point of what Levinas is trying to say, which is that subjectivity is an ethical event, something that might happen, but where there is never a guarantee that it will happen. And this is because responsibility is not something that we can force upon others; it is only something we can take upon ourselves. One could say, therefore, that Levinas leaves us educators empty-handed, as no program of action follows from his insights. Yet this empty-handedness is not necessarily a bad thing, because it precisely puts us in a position where we realize that our educational interest in the emergence of subjectivity is not to be understood in terms of production, in terms of strong, metaphysical creation, but rather requires a different kind of educational response and a different kind of educational responsibility.

If the possibility of subjectivity, the possibility of the event of subjectivity, has to do with those situations in which we are called, in which we are singled out, in which we are assigned to take responsibility for our responsibility, then one of the important things for educators to do is to make sure that our educational arrangements—our curricula, our pedagogies, our lesson plans, the ways in which we run and build our schools, and the ways in which we organize schooling in our societies—do not keep our students away from such experiences, do not shield them from any potential intervention of the other, do not contribute to making our students deaf and blind for what is calling them. Doing so will not guarantee anything, of course, other than that it will not block the event of subjectivity. But whether this event will occur, whether students will realize their subject-ness, is an entirely open question. It is beyond our control and fundamentally out of our hands. Keeping education open for the event of subjectivity to occur does, of course, come with a risk, because when we keep education open anything can happen, anything can arrive. But that is precisely the point of the argument put forward in this chapter, in that it is only when we are willing to take this risk that the event of subjectivity has a chance to occur.

CONCLUSIONS

In this chapter I have explored what it means to create and, more explicitly, what it would mean to contribute educationally to the creation of human subjectivity or subject-ness. Against a strong metaphysical conception of creation as bringing being into existence, I have, with the help of Caputo's deconstructive reading of the creation narratives in the book of Genesis, pursued a weak notion of creation as calling being into life. Here creation ceases to be a movement from non-being into being and becomes a movement "from being to the good," as Caputo puts it. Creation thus becomes an act of *affirmation* that gives what is there—the "elements," in the broadest sense of the term—significance and meaning, not a cause or a metaphysical explanation.

The two creation stories not only provide us with two very different accounts of what it means to create—a strong, metaphysical account and a weak, existential account. They also provide us with two very different accounts of what it means to educate and, more specifically, what it means to educate with an orientation toward and an interest in the event of subjectivity. The story of Yahweh not only shows us an educator who wants to stay in control and wants to minimize or even eradicate any possible risk involved in the act of creation. The story also shows what the ultimate consequence of such a risk-averse educational attitude is. Because Yahweh is not willing to take a risk, his creatures are being prevented from growing up, are being prevented from becoming subjects in their own right, from realizing their unique and singular subject-ness. Elohim, in comparison, shows us an educator who knows that creation is a risky business and has to be a risky business and that without the risk nothing will happen; the event of subjectivity will not occur.

Reading Caputo and Levinas together thus provides us with a first insight into how and why the weakness of education matters, particularly in relation to the subjectification dimension of education, that is, to the way in which education contributes to the occurrence of the event of subjectivity. While it is clear that educators cannot produce this event in the strong metaphysical sense of the word, taking the risk, keeping things open so that the event of subjectivity may arise, is nonetheless a creative gesture and a gesture of creation, albeit in the weak, existential sense in which being is brought into life—a life shared with others in responsiveness and responsibility.

CHAPTER TWO

Communication

Of all affairs, communication is the most wonderful.

—John Dewey

In the previous chapter I have explored the distinction between two understandings of creation: a strong metaphysical approach and a weak existential approach. The first is about a domain in which force matters and matter is forced; the second is about a domain of meaning, significance, morality, and ethics. If the first is about being, the second is about life; if the first is about essence, the second is about existence. Against this background I have presented an understanding of subjectivity as an event—an ethical event—in order to show how we might understand what it means not simply to have an educational interest in subjectivity and subject-ness but actually to think of education as a process that in some way contributes to the creation of such subjectivity. This, as I have shown, is not a process that operates in a strong metaphysical way, but can only be understood in weak terms—and hence has to be conceived as a process that is radically open and therefore always entails the risk that what it sets out to achieve will not be achieved. Yet this risk is necessary in order for the event of subjectivity to be able to occur, because as soon as we try to produce subjectivity, as soon as we try to control the emergence of subjectivity, it will not occur at all.

In this chapter I continue my exploration of the weak character of education through a discussion of the theme of communication. That this is an important educational theme can be gleaned from the fact that most if not all education operates through communication, be it in oral or written form or as nonverbal communication. The prevailing idea about communication—one that has strongly influenced views about what education is about—sees communication as the transmission of information from one person to another or, in more abstract terms, from one location to another. This has not only led to the widely held idea of education as a process of transmission but has also resulted in the idea that successful communication—and hence successful education—is the situation in which information is transported from one location to another without any transformation or distortion. While such a definition of successful communication may be applicable to the transmission of television signals from the studio to the living room, I will argue in this chapter that this account falls short where it concerns communication between human beings, as this is not a process of transportation of information from one mind to another, but is rather to be understood as a process of meaning and interpretation. It is a process that is radically open and undetermined—and hence weak and risky.

My discussion partners in this chapter are John Dewey and Jacques Derrida. Dewey's work is relevant because he has not only exposed the limitations of the transmission metaphor as an account of human communication but has also developed an alternative account in which communication appears as a practical, open, generative, and creative process. While Dewey's ideas are therefore important for challenging simplistic ideas about educational communication, I turn to Derrida in order to articulate a more radical and more consistent account of the openness of communication, one that takes the open and generative character of communication seriously not only at the level of theory but also at the level of theorizing, so as not to make the mistake that we can say what communication is outside of the confines of communication itself. I refer to the approach that emerges from this discussion as *deconstructive pragmatism* and suggest how deconstructive pragmatism, as a radically weak understanding of communication, might be educationally relevant.

PRAGMATISM AS A PHILOSOPHY OF COMMUNICATION

Dewey's philosophy of communication is most explicitly discussed in his book *Experience and Nature* (Dewey 1958 [1929]), particularly in chapter 5, entitled "Nature, Communication and Meaning." When Dewey opened this chapter with the statement that "of all affairs, communication is the most wonderful" (p. 166), it was not because he had found a new topic to philosophize about, but because he had come to the conclusion that mind, consciousness, thinking, subjectivity, meaning, intelligence, language, rationality, logic, inference, and truth—all those things that philosophers over the centuries have considered to be part of the natural makeup of human beings—only come into existence through and as a result of communication. "When communication occurs," Dewey thus wrote, "all natural events are subject to reconsideration and revision; they are re-adapted to meet the requirements of conversation, whether it be public discourse or that preliminary discourse termed thinking" (ibid.).

Chapter 5 of *Experience and Nature* contains many passages that exemplify the "communicative turn" in Dewey's philosophy. Dewey introduced his position by noting that "social interaction and institutions have been treated as the products of a ready-made *specific* physical or mental endowment of a self-sufficient individual" (ibid., p. 169; emphasis in original). Dewey, however, started at the other end of the equation by arguing that "the world of inner experience is dependent upon an extension of language which is a social product and operation" (ibid., p. 173). This means that "psychic events ... have language for one of their conditions" (ibid., p. 169). In Dewey's view language is itself "a natural function of human association," and its consequences "react upon other events, physical and human, giving them meaning or significance" (ibid., p. 173). Failure to see this, so Dewey argued, has led to the "subjectivistic, solipsistic and egotistic strain in modern thought" (ibid., p. 173). Yet for Dewey "soliloquy is the product and reflect of converse with others; social communication [is] not an effect of soliloquy" (ibid., p. 170), which ultimately means that "communication is a condition of consciousness" (ibid., p. 187). "If we had not talked with others and they with us, we should never talk to and with ourselves" (ibid.). Along similar lines Dewey argued that "the import of logical and rational essences is the consequence of social interactions" (ibid., p. 171), just as intelligence and meaning should be seen as "natural consequences of the peculiar form which interaction sometimes assumes in the case of human beings" (ibid., p. 180).

Dewey was well aware that putting communication at the center and beginning of his philosophy implied that he had to think differently about the process of communication itself. He could no longer rely on the idea that communication "acts as a mechanical go-between to convey observations and ideas that have prior and independent existence" (ibid., p. 169)—an idea still prevalent in our times, for example, in the idea of education as a process of transmission. This is why in *Experience and Nature* he presented a theory of communication in which communication is not seen as the transportation of information from one mind to another, but where it is understood in thoroughly *practical* terms, that is, as he put it, "as the establishment of cooperation in an activity in which there are partners, and in which the activity of each is modified and regulated by partnership" (ibid., p. 179). Against this background he defined communication as the process in which "something is literally made in common in at least two different centers of behavior" (ibid., p. 178). Communication for Dewey is a process in which person *A* and person *B* coordinate their actions around a thing in such a way that "*B*'s understanding of *A*'s movement and sounds is that he responds to the thing from the standpoint of *A*," that is, perceiving the thing "as it may function in *A*'s experience, instead of just ego-centrically" (ibid., p. 178). In this situation *B* responds to the *meaning* of *A*'s movement and sounds, rather than to the movement and sounds itself. Similarly, "*A* . . . conceives the thing not only in its direct relationship to himself, but as a thing capable of being grasped and handled by *B*. He sees the thing as it may function in *B*'s experience" (ibid.).

This view of communication as a meaningful or, better, a *meaning-guided* and *meaning-generating* process, led Dewey to the conclusion that meaning itself "is primarily a property of behavior," but the behavior of which it is a quality "is a distinctive behavior; cooperative, in that response to another's act involves contemporaneous response to a thing as entering into the other's behavior, and this upon both sides" (ibid., p. 179). It is this process, so Dewey argued, that effects "the transformation of organic gestures and cries into . . . things with significance" (ibid., p. 176) or, as he put it elsewhere, into events with meaning.

EDUCATION AS COMMUNICATION

Communication not only plays a crucial role in Dewey's general philosophical outlook—which is why I have characterized his philosophy as a philosophy of communication or, since Dewey conceives of communication in thoroughly practical terms, as a *philosophy of communicative action* (see Biesta 1994). Communication is also the central notion in Dewey's understanding of education, and, as I have argued elsewhere in detail (Biesta 2006b), a case can even be made that Dewey developed his philosophy of communication first of all in order to address educational questions, particularly how education, roughly understood as the interaction between teachers and students, is possible.

The reason Dewey approached this question neither in terms of a theory of teaching nor in terms of a theory of learning can be found in some of Dewey's earliest publications on education. In these publications he framed the question of education—or, as he put it, the *problem* of education—as the question of the *coordination* of what he termed individual and social factors. In the *Plan of Organization of the University Primary School* he wrote, "The ultimate problem of all education is to co-ordinate the psychological and the social factors" (Dewey 1895, p. 224). Some years later, in *My Pedagogic Creed* (1897), he argued along similar lines that "the psychological and social sides [of the educational process] are organically related," so that "education cannot be regarded as a compromise between the two, or a superimposition of one upon the other" (Dewey 1897, p. 85). Dewey's theory of education as communication, which was first presented in his 1916 book *Democracy and Education* (see Biesta 2006b), can be seen as a direct answer to this question, that is, how the interplay between "the child" and "the curriculum" can be brought about.

In the first three chapters of *Democracy and Education* Dewey focused this discussion on the question of how meaning can be communicated. Although he wrote that "education consists primarily in transmission through communication" (Dewey 1916, p. 12), he hastened to add that this is not a process of "direct contagion" or "literal inculcation" (ibid., p. 14). Communication should rather be understood as "a process of sharing experience till it becomes a common possession" (ibid., p. 12). This means that for Dewey the central educational "mechanism" is *participation,* or, to be more precise, "the communication which insures participation in a common understanding" (ibid., p. 7). The latter point is crucial for Dewey. Participation is neither about physical proximity nor about the situation in which all work toward a common end (see ibid., pp. 7–8). It is only when all "are *cognizant* of the common end and all [are] interested in it" that there is real participation, and it is only this kind of participation "which modifies the disposition of both parties who undertake it" (ibid., p. 12; emphasis added). This means that for Dewey education does not simply follow from *being in* a social environment. Education follows from *having* a social environment, and to have a social environment means to be in a situation in which one's activities "are associated with others" (ibid., p. 15). As Dewey explained, "A being connected with other beings cannot perform his own activities without taking the activities of others into account. For they are the indispensable conditions of the realization of his tendencies" (ibid., p. 16).

It is along these lines that Dewey suggested a crucial difference between *education* and *training.* Training is about those situations in which those who learn do not really share in the use to which their actions are put. They are not a *partner* in a shared activity. Education, in contrast, is about those situations in which one really shares or participates in a common activity, in which one really has an interest in its accomplishment just as others have. In those situations one's ideas and emotions are changed as a result of the participation. In such situations "[one] not merely acts in a way agreeing with the actions of others, but, in so acting, the same ideas and emotions are aroused in [oneself] that animate the others" (ibid., p. 17). It is not, therefore, that meaning is transmitted from one person to another. It is because people share in a common activity that their ideas and emotions are transformed as a result of and in function of the activity in which they participate. For Dewey this is the way in which things are literally made in common. "Understanding one another means that objects, including sounds, have the same value for both with respect to carrying on a common pursuit" (ibid., p. 19).

A crucial point in Dewey's account of communication is that common understanding is *not* to be seen as a condition for cooperation. It is not that we first need to come to a common understanding and only then can begin to coordinate our actions. For Dewey it is precisely the other way around: common understanding is produced by, is the outcome of successful cooperation in action. This is why he wrote that "the bare fact that language consists of sounds which are *mutually intelligible* is enough of itself to show that its meaning depends upon connections with a shared experience" (ibid., p. 19). In this respect, Dewey argued, there is no difference between the way in which the thing *hat* and the sound *h-a-t* get their meaning. Both get their meaning "by being used in a given way, and they acquire the same meaning with the child which they have with the adult because they are used in a common experience by both" (ibid., p. 19). In sum, "The guarantee for the same manner of use is found in the fact that the thing and the sounds are first employed in a *joint* activity, as a means of setting up an active connection between the child and a grown-up. Similar ideas or meanings spring up because both persons are engaged as partners in an action where what each does depends upon and influences what the other does" (ibid.; emphasis in original).

A SOCIAL THEORY OF MEANING

In *Democracy and Education* the theory of communication not only figures in Dewey's account of how meaning can be communicated. It also provides the framework for a social or communicative *theory of meaning* itself. While participation in a joint activity is central in Dewey's account of communication, he emphasized the importance of the role played by things—both the (physical) things around which action is coordinated and the sounds and gestures that are used in the coordination of action. Dewey noted that it is often argued "that a person learns by merely having the qualities of things impressed upon his mind through the gateway of the senses. Having received a store of sensory impressions, associations or some power of mental synthesis is supposed to combine them into ideas—into things with a *meaning*" (ibid., p. 34). But the meaning of stones, oranges, trees, and chairs is not to be found in the things themselves. As a matter of fact "it is the characteristic *use* to which the thing is put ... which supplies the meaning with which it is identified" (ibid., p. 34). And to have the same ideas about things that others have is "to attach the same meanings to things and to acts which others attach" (ibid., p. 35)—something that is precisely brought about through communication, through conjoint action.

Dewey's ideas about the social origin of meaning also imply that reflection itself has a social origin, in that reflection only becomes possible once one is able to make a conscious distinction between things and their possible meanings. "The difference between an adjustment to a physical stimulus and a *mental* act," Dewey wrote, "is that the latter involves a response to a thing in its *meaning*; the former does not." This gives one's behavior "a mental quality" (Dewey 1916, p. 34). And it is only when one has an *idea* of a thing that one is able "to respond to the thing in view of its place in an inclusive scheme of action" (ibid., p. 35). It becomes possible "to foresee the drift and possible consequences of the action of the thing upon us and of our action upon it" (ibid.), and this makes the transition from action to intelligent action possible—itself a crucial transition in Dewey's educational thought.

EDUCATION, COMMUNICATION, AND PARTICIPATION

The educational significance of Dewey's communicative theory of meaning is first and foremost to be found in a rejection of the idea that the child can simply discover the meaning of the world—and of the things and events in the world—through careful observation from the "outside." For Dewey the meaning of the world is, after all, not located in the things and events themselves, but in the social practices in which things, gestures, sounds, and events play a role. We could therefore say that because meaning only exists *in* social practices, it is, in a sense, located *in-between* those who constitute the social practice through their interactions. This is why communication is not about the transportation of information from point A to point B, but all about participation.

If it is the case that meaning only exists *in* social practices, then it also follows that meaning can only be (re)presented in and through social practices. For education this implies, among other things, that we should approach questions about the curriculum in terms of the representation of *practices* inside the walls of the school and not in terms of the representation of formal abstractions of these practices. This means, for example, that the teaching of mathematics should be about bringing the practice of *mathematizing* into the school and allowing for students to take part in this practice, just as, for example, the teaching of history should be about engaging students with the practice of *historizing.*

The educational implications of the participatory theory of communication are not only programmatic in that they suggest how education might be organized. The idea that students learn from the practices in which they take part is also helpful in understanding why the hidden curriculum is so effective—and often far more effective than the official curriculum. The hidden curriculum is, after all, located in the very practices in which children and students take part during their time in school, while the official curriculum is a much more artificial add-on to the real "life in schools." This also explains why one of the things that children and students learn most effectively during their time in schools and other educational institutions is the practice of schooling itself, that is, how to be a "proper" student and how to "play" the "game" of schooling.

What is unique about Dewey's theory is first and foremost the simple fact that he approaches education as a process of communication. Dewey does not focus exclusively on questions about teaching or instruction. He does not conceive, in other words, of education as something that is done *to* children and students. Instead he suggests an approach in which education is seen as something educators and students do together. But Dewey also doesn't end up in the other extreme, that is, in a theory of learning-without-teachers. While Dewey does acknowledge the crucial role of the activities of the student in the educational process, it is the configuration of this process as a process of *communication*—of participation in a *conjoint* activity—that is the central idea in Dewey's educational theory. Dewey's philosophy of education is therefore neither child-centered nor curriculum-centered but is a thoroughly *communication-centered* approach.

The central notion in this approach is the idea of *participation.* It is important to see that Dewey's views about participation are not simply meant to make clear how people learn as a result of their participation in social practices. Dewey's point is a more precise one in that he suggests that participation has the potential to generate *a particular kind of learning,* namely, the learning that leads to a transformation of ideas, emotions, and understanding of all who take part in an activity in such a way that a common or shared outlook emerges. Participation for Dewey is, however, not about physical proximity or about situations in which all simply work (or are made to work) toward a common end. For Dewey there is only (real) participation if all participants are cognizant of the common end of the activity *and* have a real interest in it. This is where the difference between *being in* a social environment and *having* a social environment is located. The upshot of this is that it is not participation as such that counts, but the *quality* of the participation. There is, in other words, educative and noneducative participation: participation in which only one party learns (by adapting to the other party), and participation that transforms the outlook of *all* who take part in it and that brings about a shared outlook.[1]

The idea that it is the quality of participation that matters is reflected in Dewey's views about democracy. In *Democracy and Education* Dewey argues that a social group in which there are many different interests and in which there is full and free interplay with other forms of association is to be preferred over a social group that is isolated from other groups and that is only held together by a limited number of interests. In the former kind of association there are many opportunities for individuals to learn and grow, while in the latter these opportunities are limited and restricted. The education such a society gives, Dewey writes, is "partial and distorted" (Dewey 1916, p. 89). A group or society, in comparison, in which many interests are shared and in which there is "free and full interplay with other forms of association," (ibid.) secures a "liberation of powers" (ibid., p. 93). The "widening of the area of shared concerns" and the "liberation of a greater diversity of personal capacities" are precisely what characterizes a "democratically constituted society" (ibid.).

SHARED WORLDS

The most important practical implication of these ideas follows from Dewey's insight that common understanding is not a precondition for human cooperation but should rather be seen as the outcome of it. It is not, as I have shown above, that we first need to come to a common understanding and only then can begin to coordinate our activities. In Dewey's view action comes first and the transformation of understanding follows from it. Yet these ideas should be read in conjunction with Dewey's understanding of participation. Whereas it might be claimed that all participation will result in a change of outlook, there is an important difference between forms of collective action in which people work toward a common end but have no stake in it—where, in other words, the agenda for the activity is set by others—and those forms of collective action in which all who take part have an interest in the activity and can contribute

---

1. In my view this is precisely the difference between Dewey's ideas about learning through participation and the theory of learning through participation put forward by Lave and Wenger in their 1991 book *Situated Learning*.

to decisions about its direction. Dewey's claim is that it is only the latter form of collective action that will bring about a shared outlook and understanding and, ultimately, a shared and common (but not necessarily identical) world.

This line of thought is first of all important for our understanding of the role of schools in society. Whereas many would argue that the prime function of schools is to create a common outlook *so that* future collective action becomes possible, Dewey suggests that schools should instead focus on the creation of opportunities for participation in order for such a shared outlook to emerge. Yet not any form of participation will do. The creation of a shared outlook will not result from simple coexistence or from forms of pseudo-participation in which the activity is set and controlled by others. It will only result from participation in activities in which all who take part have a stake in the activity. This, therefore, is not simply an argument for comprehensive schooling—although it is this as well. It is first and foremost an argument for what we might call the internal democratization of schooling, that is, for a kind of education in which all who take part, teachers and students, have a real interest and a real stake. It may be difficult to achieve this—and some might even argue that democracy and schooling are by definition incompatible—yet Dewey at least helps us to see the challenge entailed in the idea of democratic schooling.

The importance of Dewey's ideas about the relationship between participation and learning are, however, not confined to educational institutions. They also have something important to contribute to one of the most vexing problems of contemporary life: the question of how to live together in a world of plurality and difference, a world divided along the lines of class, race, gender, culture, religion, and worldview. Dewey, so we could say, is a great believer in the contact hypothesis, the idea that the only way to overcome differences—or to be more precise, to bring about communication across differences—is by bringing people together. Dewey helps us to see, however, that not any form of contact will do but that what matters is the *quality* of the contact. And the key word, again, is *participation,* that is, that form of collective action in which all who take part have a stake. Although our world of global media and Internet suggests that there is much more communication—or at least that there are many more opportunities for communication—than there were in the past, Dewey helps us to see that such communication is not automatically participation, which helps to understand why communication across differences seems to have become *more* problematic rather than less. The creation of a shared world requires, after all, that all who take part have an interest and a stake, but precisely this is often lacking, for example, in the interaction between the so-called first and third world or in the interaction between different classes or different cultures or religions. While Dewey does not provide an easy way out, his understanding of communication-as-participation does have something important to offer, both as an analytical framework and as an agenda for action.

What is also important for the overall argument I am pursuing in this book is that Dewey provides us with a *weak* understanding of communication, that is, of communication as a process that is not only radically open and undetermined but also generative and creative. For Dewey communication is a process in which meaning is made and shared, not a mechanical "go-between" for the "safe" transportation of bits of information from one location to another. With Dewey communication thus emerges as an encounter between subjects, not an exchange between objects—so that it comes with all the risk and unpredictability that is at stake in such encounters.

A METAPHYSICS OF PRESENCE?

Whereas the implications of Dewey's philosophy of communication are impressive and noteworthy, the philosophical framework from which these ideas emerge is itself not without problems—at least not, so I wish to argue, without *philosophical* problems. One of the key questions is whether these philosophical problems translate into practical problems. Pragmatists might argue that at the end of the day the only thing that really counts are the *consequences* of Dewey's philosophy of communication, not its foundations. I wish to argue, however, that the foundations of Dewey's philosophy in a sense "trouble" its consequences, and it is for this reason that a critical examination of these foundations is called for. So what is the problem?

One way to approach the issue is to go back to the ambition of Dewey's philosophy. As I have shown, Dewey's philosophy can be understood as an attempt to overcome the (modern) philosophy of consciousness by providing a new starting point for philosophy, a starting point called "communication." This lies behind Dewey's claim that communication is a condition of consciousness rather than that consciousness is a condition of communication. Notwithstanding the radical implications of this "Gestalt switch," it is important to see that what is at stake in this switch is a *replacement* of one starting point for philosophy—consciousness—with another starting point—communication. Several commentators have observed that there is an important qualitative difference between both starting points. With regard to this I am inclined to agree with Garrison (1999) that the shift from consciousness to communication entails a shift from a "metaphysics of *essence*," a metaphysics of original and ultimate "things," to a "metaphysics of *existence*," a metaphysics of process and being (see also Sleeper 1986). While this does signal a move away from traditional essentialist metaphysics, I do *not* think—unlike Garrison (1999, p. 358)—that the shift from essence to existence also implies a move away from a "metaphysics of *presence*."

It is here that there is an important difference between Dewey's critique of metaphysics and the one that can be found in the writings of Jacques Derrida. Whereas Dewey's critique is aimed at a particular *type* of metaphysics, namely essentialist metaphysics, Derrida's critique is not aimed at a particular type of metaphysics but is a questioning of the metaphysical "gesture" itself—a questioning of the very *possibility* of metaphysics. The central notion in this questioning is the idea of the "metaphysics of presence." Derrida's argument here is that the history of Western philosophy can be understood as a continuous attempt to locate a fundamental ground, a fixed center, an Archimedean point, which serves both as an absolute beginning and as a center from which everything originating from it can be mastered and controlled (see Derrida 1978, p. 279). He claims that ever since Plato this origin has been defined in terms of *presence*, that is, as an origin that is self-sufficient and fully present to itself; an origin that simply "exists." For Derrida, therefore, the "determination of Being as *presence*" is the very matrix of the history of metaphysics, and this history coincides with the history of the West in general (see ibid., p. 279). "It could be shown," he writes, "that all the names related to fundamentals, to principles, or to the center have always designated an invariable presence" (ibid.). Here we should not only think of such apparent fundamentals as "God" or "nature." For Derrida *any* attempt to present something as original, fundamental, and self-sufficient—and for Derrida this includes both "consciousness" and "communication"—is an example of what he refers to as the "metaphysics of presence" (see ibid., p. 281). Derrida also emphasizes that the metaphysics of presence includes more than just the determination of the meaning of being as presence. It entails a *hierarchical axiology* in which the origin is designated as pure, simple, normal, standard, self-sufficient, and self-identical, which means that everything that follows from it can only be understood in terms of derivation, complication, deterioration, accident, and so on.

Why is the metaphysics of presence a problem? This is actually not an easy question to answer. In a sense Derrida's whole oeuvre can be seen as a series of attempts to answer this question *and*—and the "and" is very important here—to reflect on how and from where this question might be answered (see Biesta 2001, 2003). One approach to this question centers on the observation that presence always requires the "help" of something that is not present, that is, something that is absent. The point Derrida makes here is that what is "present" is constituted "by means of [the] very relation to what it is not" (Derrida 1982, p. 13). "Good," for example, only has meaning because it is different from "evil." One might argue that "good" is originary and that "evil" is secondary and has to be understood as a lapse or fall, as the absence of good. But as soon as we try to define "good" without any recourse whatsoever to a notion of evil, it becomes clear that the presence of "good" is only possible because of its relationship to what is not good, namely, "evil" (for this example see Lucy 2004, p. 102). This shows that the "contamination" of good by evil is a *necessary* contamination, as Derrida would put it. Stated in more general terms it reveals that the "otherness" that is excluded to maintain the myth of a pure and uncontaminated original presence is actually constitutive of that which presents itself as such. We could say that the "thing" that makes "good" possible (i.e., "evil") is the very "thing" that also undermines it and makes it impossible. It is this strange "logic" where a condition of possibility is at the very same time a condition of impossibility to which Derrida sometimes refers as *deconstruction*.

It is important to see what deconstruction is and what it is not. Deconstruction, to put it simply, is *not* the activity of revealing the impossibility of metaphysics. It also isn't something that Derrida does or that other philosophers can do (which is why, from a technical-philosophical perspective, it is a little unfortunate that so many people now use the word *deconstruct* when they actually mean something like *analyze*). Derrida explains that

> "deconstructions," which I prefer to say in the plural ... is one of the possible names to designate ... what occurs [*ce qui arrive*], or cannot manage to occur [*ce qui n'arrive pas à arriver*], namely a certain dislocation, which in effect reiterates itself regularly—and wherever there is something rather than nothing. (Derrida and Ewald 2001, p. 67)

Deconstruction, therefore, is "not a method and cannot be transformed into one" (Derrida 1991, p. 273), which means that all deconstruction is "auto-deconstruction" (see Derrida 1997, p. 9). What one can do, however, and what Derrida has done many times in his writings, is to show, to reveal, or as Bennington (2000, p. 11) puts it, to *witness* deconstruction or, to be more precise, to witness *metaphysics-in-deconstruction*. Whereas witnessing metaphysics-in-deconstruction reveals the impossibility of the metaphysics of presence and hence the possibility of all metaphysics—because presence always needs absence just as identity always presupposes alterity—the act of witnessing is not what the word *deconstruction* refers to. Deconstruction is, in other words, not something that people do; it is something that occurs (or, as

Derrida would have it, also cannot manage to occur). To witness metaphysics-in-deconstruction is therefore, as Derrida has put it, about challenging "the authority of the 'is'" (Derrida, quoted in Lucy 2004, p. 12).

WITNESSING DECONSTRUCTION

Why might it be important to witness metaphysics-in-deconstruction? The most straightforward answer to this question is that we should do this in order to do justice to what is made invisible by the metaphysics of presence but yet is necessary to make this presence possible. It is to do justice to what is excluded by what is present. It is to do justice to the "other" of presence. This already suggests that the point of deconstruction is not negative or destructive but first and foremost *affirmative* (see Derrida 1997, p. 5). It is an affirmation of what is excluded and forgotten, an affirmation of what is *other*. Another way of putting this is to say that deconstruction wants to open up the metaphysics of presence—or, for that matter any system—in the name of what cannot be thought of in terms of the system and yet makes the system possible. This reveals that the point of deconstruction is not simply to affirm what is *known* to be excluded by the system. What is at stake in witnessing metaphysics-in-deconstruction is an affirmation of what is wholly other, of what is unforeseeable from the present. It is, as Derrida puts it, an affirmation of an otherness that is always to come, as an event that "as event, exceeds calculation, rules, programs, anticipations" (Derrida 1992b, p. 27). In this sense it is not simply an affirmation of who or what is other, but rather of the *otherness* of who or what is other. Deconstruction, as Caputo has summarized, is an opening and an openness toward an *unforeseeable* in-coming of the other (see Caputo 1997, p. 42). This is what Derrida sometimes has referred to as "the impossible"—which is not what is not possible but what cannot be foreseen as a possibility.

It is important to see that all this does *not* amount to an attempt to overcome, to do away with, or to destruct metaphysics. Whereas Derrida wants to put the metaphysical "gesture" of Western philosophy into question, he states that his approach is different from Nietzsche's "demolition" of metaphysics or Heidegger's "destruction" (*Destruktion* or *Abbau*) (see Derrida 1991, pp. 270–271). Nietzsche, Heidegger, and all the other "destructive discourses" within Western thought wanted to make a total break with the metaphysical tradition. They wanted to end and to overcome metaphysics. Derrida believes, however, that such a total rupture is not a real possibility because if we would leave metaphysics behind, we would have nothing to stand on and no tool to work with. He explains,

> There is no sense in doing without the concepts of metaphysics in order to shake metaphysics. We ... can pronounce not a single destructive proposition which has not already had to slip into the form, the logic, and the implicit postulations of precisely what it seeks to contest. (Derrida 1978, p. 280)

While Derrida wants to "shake" metaphysics, he thus acknowledges that this cannot be done from some neutral and innocent place "outside" of metaphysics. He acknowledges that we cannot step outside of the tradition, since that would leave us without any tools, without even a language to investigate, criticize, and "shake" metaphysics—it would even leave us without a place to stand. What is more to the point, therefore, is to say—in simple words—that Derrida wants to shake metaphysics by showing that it is itself always already "shaking," by showing, in other words, the impossibility of any of its attempts to fix or immobilize being through the presentation of a self-sufficient, self-identical presence, by witnessing metaphysics-in-deconstruction. The act of witnessing can, however, only be performed from the "inside"—or at least *not* from some kind of neutral, uncontaminated position outside of the system. In this respect Derrida clearly rejects the traditional philosophical "position" of the philosopher as the outside-spectator, the one who oversees the universe without being part of it. For Derrida one of the key questions is precisely the question "from what site or non-site (*non-lieu*) philosophy [can] as such appear to itself as other than itself, so that it can interrogate and reflect upon itself in an original manner" (Derrida 1984, p. 108).

DECONSTRUCTION IN PRAGMATISM, PRAGMATISM IN DECONSTRUCTION

How do these considerations affect Dewey's philosophy of communication-as-participation? At a philosophical level they help to make visible that Dewey's shift from consciousness to communication does not at all imply a move away from the metaphysics of *presence*. To claim that "communication is a condition of consciousness" (Dewey 1958 [1929], p. 187) and to use this idea as the framework for reconsidering mind, thinking, meaning, intelligence, language, rationality, logic, inference, and truth—all those things that philosophers over the centuries have considered to be part of the natural makeup of the human being—is clearly a metaphysical "move" in that it is an attempt to identify a first principle, an origin from which everything else follows. Although Dewey's is not a metaphysics of *essence* but rather a metaphysics of *existence* in that Dewey starts his philosophizing from a process—communication—not a "thing" or substance, it is a metaphysics nonetheless—a metaphysics that posits communication as the most original phenomenon, the "presence" from which everything else derives.

Should this be a problem? Dewey's most pragmatic readers might say that as long as "communication" generates more interesting consequences than "consciousness" we should go for the former. If "communication"—and they might even say, if a *metaphysics* of communication—provides us with better tools to address key problems in education, democracy, and society, then we should use it until more useful tools come around. Such readers might find Derrida's suggestion that there is a philosophical problem with positing communication as a self-sufficient origin is an interesting theoretical observation, but probably an observation that is rather remote from the real problems to which they wish to devote their attention. But if Derrida is right in claiming that any attempt to be metaphysical relies on the exclusion of something that makes the illusion of self-sufficient presence possible, then there is a real need to examine whether Dewey's philosophy of communication "produces" any exclusions—not in the least because the overt intention of this philosophy is to be inclusive rather than exclusive.

One point where I do believe that Dewey's philosophy of communication may not only produce exclusion but may also work against its own intentions has to do with the fact that his philosophy is based upon a Western, naturalistic, and secular worldview. It is a worldview that says that human beings are the outcome of a long evolutionary trajectory and that the "intervention" of communication in this trajectory has made us who we are. While this may be a set of acceptable assumptions for some—and in such cases there is perhaps no problem in using Dewey's philosophy of communication to inform educational and democratic practices—is it *not* a set of assumptions that is universally shared and accepted. This immediately raises the question whether this philosophy can really facilitate communication across differences or whether it can only facilitate communication among those who share a similar set of assumptions about the world and their place in it. How, in other words, can we utilize Dewey's philosophy in our communication with those who do not believe in the worldview that underlies and informs this philosophy (on this problem see also Festenstein 1997)?

This remains a problem as long as we approach Dewey's philosophy of communication in the traditional philosophical—or metaphysical—way, that is, as a description of "the human condition" from the outside. If, however, we take the communicative *intention* of this philosophy seriously, then it means that we can no longer think of this philosophy as a philosophy that describes and in a sense circumscribes our communicative practices from the outside.

This means that the only way in which we can take the communicative ethos of pragmatism seriously is if we enter this approach in our communication with others. We should no longer think of it, therefore, as a kind of "meta-theory" that describes communication from the outside and that in this sense can come before communication. The only way in which we can take this theory seriously is if we offer it in our communication with others as a possible position, a possible way to understand communication.

The idea of "offering" has to be taken quite literally though, because, as Dewey knows all too well, communication always entails the risk of change and transformation. In a sense, communication can only exist in and through transformation—which means, in Derrida's terms, that communication is always already *in deconstruction*. To be serious about Dewey's philosophy of communication therefore means that we must be prepared to take the risk that this philosophy will change as a result of our entering this philosophy in our communication with others. As long as we try to preclude this risk we are not engaging in a process that on Dewey's definition would count as real communication and real participation; and in doing so we would preclude the opportunity for our partners in communication to appear as other than what our theories, assumptions, and expectations may want them to be.

This not only means that the only possibility for communication lies in its deconstruction—that is, in the acknowledgment that communication is a weak, open, and risky process, a process that is only made possible by taking the radical openness and unpredictability of all communication seriously. It also means that the only possibility for a philosophy or theory of communication lies in its deconstruction, that is, in the acknowledgment that such a philosophy or theory can never fix or determine what communication is or should be about, but can ultimately only be offered in communication. That is why I wish to suggest that the only possible future for pragmatism has to be as a deconstructive pragmatism. Deconstructive pragmatism is not a deconstructed pragmatism—it is not a pragmatism that is destructed or destroyed—but rather a pragmatism that acknowledges the fact that it is always in deconstruction because it can only exist in communication.

CONCLUSIONS

In this chapter I have engaged in a discussion between pragmatism and deconstruction. I have tried to make clear why I believe that pragmatism's philosophy of communication still has important things to say about educative processes in plural societies, particularly with respect to questions about communication across differences. The main message that follows from Dewey's practical view of communication—communication as something we *do*—is that the starting point for communication lies in participation, that is, in doing things *together*. Dewey also shows, however, that it is the *quality* of participation that counts, which means that only forms of participation in which all have an interest and a stake have the potential to contribute to the ongoing creation of a shared world (which, to make the point one more time, is not a world in which everyone has an identical outlook but a world in which everyone can take part in their own ways). As I have mentioned before, this is not something that can easily be realized, but Dewey at least provides us with a criterion to distinguish between "real" and "pseudo" participation.

While Dewey thus makes an important contribution to understanding communication in a weak, open, and risky way—not only at the general level of the theory and philosophy of communication but also in relation to educational communication—I have indicated that there is at least a philosophical problem with Dewey's approach that has to do with its metaphysical character and, more specifically, with the fact that communication figures as an original and self-sufficient "presence" from which everything else emanates. I have tried to make clear that this is not just a philosophical problem but one that potentially has practical implications as well. The main tension here is between the communicative intent or ethos of Dewey's philosophy—his insistence that communication is an open and generative process, a process of doing things together so as to make things in common—and the particular way in which Dewey theorizes communication. The danger here, to put it briefly, is that this theory becomes a template for how communication should proceed and thus begins to close the very things it aims to open up. This is why, with Derrida, I have suggested that the communicative ethos of Dewey's philosophy needs to be approached in a deconstructive way, not only at the level of communication itself—which, if we follow Dewey, has to be understood as a process that is always already "in deconstruction"—but also with regard to the theory and philosophy of communication that we can find in Dewey's writings.

CHAPTER THREE

Teaching

Teaching is not reducible to maieutics; it comes from the exterior and
brings me more than I contain.

—*Emmanuel Levinas*

To suggest that education operates by means of communication is, in itself,
not really contentious. It is quite obvious that when education happens it
happens through communication—which does not necessarily mean that
it happens through spoken or written words alone. Things become already
a bit more interesting when we raise the question of how communication
actually "works," and in the previous chapter I have shown that it makes all
the difference whether we think of communication in logistical terms—that
is, in terms of the transportation of chunks of information from A to B—or
whether we think of it as a generative process of participation through which
things—in the widest sense of the word—are made "in common." The latter
view depicts educational communication as an open process and therefore as
a process that always entails a risk. To take the risk out of communication
would mean to turn it back into a form of transportation where communication
would lose its dialogical potential, that is, its ability to do justice to all who
take part. The question as to what it means to do justice to all who take part
in communication is not a question that can simply be resolved at the level
of theory—it is not a matter of just having the "right" theory—which means
that we ultimately also need to risk our *theories* of communication themselves.

While the deconstructive pragmatism that follows from these considerations provides important markers for educational processes and practices,

43

there is one conclusion that explicitly should *not* be drawn from the foregoing exploration of the role of communication in education, which is the suggestion that because education operates *through* communication, communication *is* education. Being involved in collective meaning making, even being involved in collective learning, is not automatically a case of education. There are a number of reasons for this—and some of these I have explored elsewhere, particularly in relation to the difference between learning and education (see Biesta 2006a, 2010b), an issue to which I will return in the next chapter. In this chapter I will focus on one particular aspect of the discussion, which has to do with teaching and the role of the teacher. Starting from the assumption that teaching is a necessary component of all education, I will explore what this means for our understanding of teaching and the teacher. Against the idea of the teacher as a fellow learner or a facilitator of learning, I will suggest that we should understand the teacher as someone who, in the most general sense, brings something new to the educational situation, something that was not already there. That is why I will suggest that teaching cannot be entirely immanent to the educational situation but requires a notion of "transcendence."

To think about teaching in terms of transcendence suggests that teaching can be understood as a gift or as an act of gift giving. I argue, however, that we shouldn't think that it lies in the power of the teacher to give the gift of teaching—and it is precisely here that we can find a weak "moment" in (our understanding of) teaching. This is why I explore the question of the gift of teaching and teaching as a gift from the other side of the spectrum, that is, in terms of what it might mean (and how it might be possible) to receive the gift of teaching. In relation to this I highlight the importance of the distinction between "learning from" and "being taught by" and suggest that it is the latter idea that might help us to reclaim teaching for education or, as I put it below, to give teaching back to education.

CONSTRUCTIVISM AND THE END OF TEACHING

If there is one idea that has significantly changed classroom practice in many countries around the world in recent decades, it has to be constructivism. For constructivism to have had such an impact, it necessarily had to become theoretically multiple and open. Thus the constructivist classroom takes inspiration from a range of different—and to a certain extent even conflicting—theories and ideas, such as the radical constructivism of Ernst von Glasersfeld, the cognitive constructivism of Jean Piaget, the social constructivism of Lev Vygotsky, and the transactional constructivism of John Dewey. What unites these approaches—at least at a superficial level—and thus generally characterizes the constructivist classroom, is an emphasis on student activity. This is based on the assumption that students have to construct their own insights, understandings, and knowledge, and that teachers cannot do this for them. In the constructivist classroom, therefore, constructivism operates not just as a learning theory or an epistemology, but also, and first and foremost, as a *pedagogy*. Virginia Richardson has correctly pointed out that "constructivism is a theory of learning and not a theory of teaching" (Richardson 2003, p. 1629). This not only means that constructivist pedagogy is not simply the application of constructivist learning theory—Richardson goes even further by arguing that "the elements of effective constructivist teaching are not known" (ibid.)—but also implies that a belief in constructivist learning theory does not necessarily require that one adopt a constructivist pedagogy. After all, "students also make meaning from activities encountered in a transmission model of teaching" (ibid., p. 1628).

Although constructivism is first of all a theory of learning, the uptake of this theory in schools, colleges, and universities has led to a change in practice that is often characterized as a shift "from teaching to learning." Barr and Tagg (1995) have made the even stronger claim that what is at stake here is a Kuhnian paradigm shift from what they refer to as the "instruction paradigm" to the "learning paradigm." The point of using these phrases is not to suggest that under the instruction paradigm there was no interest in student learning whereas under the learning paradigm there is. The point for Barr and Tagg—and for the many others who have made similar observations so as to create a present-day "common sense" about education—is that in the instruction paradigm the focus is on the transmission of content from the teacher to the student, whereas in the learning paradigm the focus is on the ways in which teachers can support and facilitate student learning. This is in line with Richardson's description of constructivist pedagogy as involving "the creation of classroom environments, activities, and methods that are grounded in a constructivist theory of learning, with goals that focus on individual students developing deep understandings in the subject matter of interest and habits of mind that aid in future learning" (Richardson 2003, p. 1627).

The shift from teaching to learning—a shift that is part of a wider "learnification" of educational discourse and practice (see also Chapter 4)—has radically changed common perceptions of what teaching entails and of what a teacher is. Constructivist thinking has, on the one hand, promoted the idea of teaching as the creation of learning environments and as facilitating, supporting, or scaffolding student learning. On the other hand it has, in one and the same move, discredited the "transmission model of teaching" and thus has given lecturing and so-called didactic teaching a really bad name.[1] Constructivism seems, in other words, to have given up on the idea that teachers have something to teach and that students have something to learn from their teachers. If I see it correctly this has even led to a certain embarrassment among teachers about the very idea of teaching and about their identity as teachers. This is, perhaps, what concerns me most, because if we give up on the idea that teachers have something to teach and make them into facilitators of learning, we do, in a sense, give up on the very idea of education.

The issue that interests me in this chapter, therefore, has to do with the impact of constructivist thinking (conceived in the broad sense outlined above) on teaching. I am interested in its impact not only on the practice of teaching but also on the role of the teacher, the identity of the teacher, the justification of the teacher "position," and even on the very idea of teaching and the very idea of the teacher. The question I wish to address is what it might take to give teaching a place again in our understanding of education, that is, to give teaching "back" to education. And the thesis I wish to explore is whether it might be that case that the idea of teaching only has meaning if it carries with it a certain idea of "transcendence," that is, if we understand teaching as something that comes radically from the outside, as something that transcends the self of the "learner," transcends the one who is being taught.

Constructivist Pedagogy, Immanence, and the Learning Paradox

The reason why teaching—or a certain conception of teaching that is not about the facilitation of learning—seems to have dropped out of the equation has to do with the fact that constructivism sees the process of learning as *immanent*. Although this already creates problems for constructivism as a theory of learning, it becomes even more of a problem when constructivism

---

1. I wish to emphasize that the phenomenon that forms the occasion for my reflections in this chapter is the way in which, through references to constructivist ideas and intuitions, the idea of teaching—and hence the idea of the teacher—seemed to have changed its meaning to such an extent that the teacher has become at most a facilitator of learning and in some cases just a fellow learner. I am therefore neither analyzing nor criticizing constructivist ideas themselves but am interested in the way in which certain conceptions of constructivism—which obviously also include *mis*conceptions—have contributed to what we might call the demise, the disappearance, or, in a more post-modern mode, the end or even the death of the teacher. For a recent critical discussion of the idea of constructivism see Roth (2011).

gets translated into a pedagogy and becomes part of a theory of education, as one could argue that the very point of education is precisely *not* to repeat what is already there but to bring something new to the scene. This is, of course, an old discussion in the educational literature, one that goes straight back to Plato's *Meno,* to Socrates, and to the learning paradox—and many authors do indeed conceive of Socrates and Plato as "the first constructivists in education" (Nola and Irzik 2005, p. 105) or, to be more precise, as the first ones enacting a constructivist *pedagogy.*[2]

The learning paradox is the predicament posed by Meno as to how one can go looking for something when one doesn't know what one is looking for, and how one can recognize what one is looking for if one doesn't know it. Meno poses the question as follows, "And how will you enquire, Socrates, into that which you do not know? What will you put forth as the subject of enquiry? And if you find what you want, how will you ever know that this is the thing which you did not know?" Socrates then reformulates the problem as follows, "I know, Meno, what you mean; but just see what a tiresome dispute you are introducing. You argue that a man cannot enquire either about that which he knows, or about that which he does not know; for if he knows, he has no need to enquire; and if not, he cannot; for he does not know the very subject about which he is to enquire."[3] Socrates's way out of the learning paradox is to argue that all learning is a matter of *recollection.* This is why he can deny that he has anything to teach and is involved in teaching. It is also why he represents his educational efforts as entirely *maieutic*: bringing out what is already there.

It is not too difficult to see the connection with constructivism, not only in terms of the theory of learning but also with regard to the vanishing role of the teacher. But whereas Socrates *says* that he is not involved in any teaching and by doing so even wishes to deny the very possibility of teaching, this is not consistent with what he actually *does.* Sharon Todd, whose argument I follow here, argues in her book *Learning from the Other* that Socrates "cannot simply be taken at his word" (Todd 2003, p. 23) and shows, through a subtle reading of the *Meno,* that there is actually quite a lot of teaching going on in the way in which Socrates tries to convince Meno's slave boy that he already possesses the knowledge he did not realize he possessed. Todd particularly

---

2. Nola and Irzik (2005) do, however, note that while Plato and Socrates can be seen as the first enacting a constructivist *pedagogy,* they do not hold a constructivist theory of knowledge.

3. Plato's *Meno,* translated by Benjamin Jowett. Project Gutenberg E-Book: www.gutenberg.org/files/1643/1643-h/1643-h.htm (last accessed June 5, 2012).

highlights the teaching performed by Socrates that has an impact on the slave boy's identity, a process through which the slave boy is being taught that he is indeed a slave boy, and also the process through which the slave boy is being taught that he is a learner, that is, a "subject of pedagogy" (ibid., p. 24). Todd thus presents Socrates as "the teacher, who, like the perfect murderer, makes it appear that teaching has not taken place, who leaves the scene without a trace, and who, moreover, is convinced of his own innocence" (ibid.). She adds, however, that by proclaiming his questions to be innocent, Socrates actually "obscures the fundamental structures of alteration and asymmetry that are present between teacher and student" (ibid., p. 25).

Todd's reading provides support for the suggestion that the idea of teaching only has meaning if it carries with it a notion of "transcendence," that is, if it is understood as something that comes from the outside and *adds* rather than that it just confirms what is already there. Her argument also shows that the shift from teaching to learning is in a sense ideological, in that it hides the teaching that goes on under the name of Socratic questioning. To highlight what I see as the transcendent dimension of teaching, Todd turns to Levinas, who indeed makes the claim that "teaching is not reducible to maieutics [but] comes from the exterior and brings me more than I contain" (Levinas 1969, p. 51). Todd explains that the view of teaching as bringing more than I contain "is antithetical to the Socratic method that so predominates dialogical approaches to educational practice, where teaching is viewed as 'bringing out of the I that which it already contains'" (Todd 2003, p. 30). This is why she concludes that "the maieutic model erases the significance of the Other and claims that learning is a recovery contained within the I, rather than a disruption of the I provoked by the Other in a moment of sociality" (ibid.).

Todd's argumentation makes an important contribution to understanding the significance of the idea of transcendence in teaching. Yet there are two aspects that, in my view, need expansion. One is relatively minor. Todd focuses her argument strongly on the idea of "learning to become"—a notion inspired by Sigmund Freud and Cornelius Castoriadis. While "becoming" may be part of what happens as a result of learning, I do not think that it is the only thing that matters in education—and to a certain extent I would even want to question the suggestion that we need to learn in order to become (see also Chapter 4). This is why I would disagree with the statement from Castoriadis, quoted by Todd, in which he argues that "the point of pedagogy is not to teach particular things, but to develop in the subject the capacity to learn" (Todd 2003, p. 19). I would like to place a stronger emphasis on the "act" of teaching and take a broader view of what the purposes of teaching can be (see also Biesta 2010b, chapter 1), which for me would include the teaching of "particular things."

The more important issue, however, has to do with the way in which the notion of "transcendence" figures in the discussion—and my point here is not to criticize Todd but to notice the particular use of this notion and then make a suggestion to take this a step further. What is interesting about Todd's discussion is that with Levinas, she does indeed engage explicitly with the idea of "transcendence." Yet this transcendence is always brought back to—or perhaps we could say contained within—the idea of the Other, understood as "a specific, embodied individual" (Todd 2003, p. 47, note 1). While Todd emphasizes that what Levinas means by the Other is neither simply "a sociological 'Other' who is marginalized or maligned" nor "another person who, as a subject, resembles myself," and while she quotes Levinas in saying that "the Other is what I myself am not" (ibid., p. 29), the Other that transcends the self, either as teacher or as another from whom we can "learn to become," only seems to figure in the discussion as a *human* other. The issue I wish to raise here is not whether this, in itself, poses a problem—one could even argue that this is precisely what is distinctive about Levinas's notion of transcendence (see below). The issue is rather whether, when we say that the other is what I myself am not, this otherness can be contained to concrete and identifiable other human beings, or whether we should be open to the possibility that something more radically different might break through. The question here is, therefore, how we might *think transcendence,* which, as I will suggest, also raises the question how we might *transcend thinking*—particularly the thinking of what "is" transcendent. It is to this question that I now turn.

THINKING TRANSCENDENCE, TRANSCENDING THINKING

My guide in extending the idea of transcendence a little is a recent book by Merold Westphal (2008) called *Levinas and Kierkegaard in Dialogue.* In the book Westphal brings the ideas of these two thinkers "in conversation" precisely around the theme of transcendence (see also Henriksen 2010). One of the central claims of the book is that both for Levinas and for Kierkegaard transcendence involves more than only the otherness of other human beings. Yet while Levinas and Kierkegaard agree "that the transcendence and alterity that deserve to be called divine are not to be found in the realm of theoretical knowledge [but] occur in the decentering of the cognitive self by a command that comes from on high," they disagree "in that Levinas insists that the neighbor is always the middle term between me and God, while Kierkegaard insists that it is God who is always the middle term between me and my neighbor" (ibid., p. 5).

In the first two chapters of his book Westphal discusses this through the notion of "revelation." What is interesting for the discussion is that Kierkegaard, under the pseudonym of Johannes Climacus, explores the idea of revelation through a discussion of the *Meno*, focusing on the question whether it is possible to think of teaching outside of, and different from, the idea of maieutics (see Kierkegaard 1985). Whereas the maieutic conception of teaching sees teaching as *accidental* to learning, Climacus asks, by way of a "thought-project" (ibid., p. 9), "what would have to be true *if* there were to be an alternative to Socrates's account of knowledge as recollection, *if* the teacher were really to teach so that the relation to the teacher would be essential rather than accidental" (Westphal 2008, p. 25). The answer Kierkegaard develops is that the teacher not only needs to give the learner the truth but also needs to give the learner "the condition of recognizing it as truth," because "if the learner were himself the condition for understanding the truth, then he merely needs to recollect" (ibid., p. 25; see also Kierkegaard 1985, p. 14). This "double truth giving" is what Climacus characterizes as *revelation*. Revelation therefore means not merely "that the teacher presents the learner with some knowledge not already possessed, but more importantly, also [with] the condition for recognizing it as truth," as it is only in the latter case that "the relation to the teacher becomes *essential*" (Westphal 2008, p. 25; emphasis added).

Climacus helps us see that a notion of teaching that is essential rather than accidental to learning is not simply about presenting students with something they do not yet know. It rather is about presenting students with something that "is neither derivable from nor validated by what [they] already know" (ibid., p. 26) but that truly transcends what they already know. As Westphal explains, "For both Kierkegaard and Levinas the knowledge that deserves to be called revelation is independent of the "already saids" that are the condition for our recognition of the truth as such" (ibid.). This is why Levinas writes that Socratic teaching is characterized by the "primacy of the same," that is, "to receive nothing of the Other but what is in me, as though from all eternity I was in possession of what comes to me from the outside" (Levinas 1969, p. 43). In contrast to this, Levinas is after a relationship in which I receive from the other "beyond the capacity of the I"—which not only means "to have an idea of infinity" but also means "to be taught" (ibid., p. 51). And it is this teaching that can be called *revelation* (ibid., p. 67).

Westphal notes that both Levinas and Kierkegaard link the notion of revelation to that of *authority*. After all, if teaching is about presenting students with something that is "neither derivable from nor validated by" what they already know, then they have to take it on the authority of the teacher. The wider significance of this insight lies in the fact that, as Westphal puts it, "for both Levinas and Kierkegaard the basis of the ethical and religious life lies in an authoritative revelation that in its immediacy comes to us from beyond our own powers of recollection" (ibid., p. 26). In the 1965 essay "Phenomenon and Enigma" (Levinas 1987), Levinas refers to this revelation as "enigma" in order to highlight that what is revealed is not a phenomenon, not something that is comprehensible and can be comprehended by me, but rather something that is "beyond" my cognition and comprehension—and therefore even "beyond being" (ibid., p. 62) and "beyond reason" (ibid., p. 61). Enigma is about a way of "manifesting oneself without manifesting oneself," as Levinas puts it. It stands for that which "signifies itself without revealing itself" (ibid., p. 73). It is about God who literally "comes to mind" (Levinas 1998b), rather than a mind trying to comprehend God.

Westphal shows that with the idea of "enigma" Levinas is both arguing against a logocentric reason that "arbitrarily excludes God from its world" and thus is "dogmatically atheistic" and a logocentric reason that "domesticates God by transforming the divine into a (visible or intelligible) phenomenon"— a process in which "the divinity of God dissipates" (Westphal 2008, p. 31). The latter point explains why Levinas's emphasis on the other—on what, above, I have referred to as the *human* other—does not exclude the possibility of "further" or "other" transcendence, so to speak. What Levinas wants to prevent is the situation in which (knowledge of) God gets in the way of my hearing the other—which, unlike Kierkegaard, he sees as a bigger problem than the option where the other would get in the way of my seeing God (see ibid., p. 53). This is what Westphal refers to as the idea of the ethical as "the teleological suspension of the religious" (ibid., p. 47). Suspension here is not to be understood as a reduction of the religious to the ethical, but as a negation of its claim to autonomy and self-sufficiency. That is why Westphal writes that "teleological suspension does not eliminate; it relativizes" (ibid.).

Westphal provides a strong argument, based on his reading of Levinas's essay "God and Philosophy" (Levinas 1998a, pp. 55–78), why transcendence matters for *philosophy*. Central to the argument is Levinas's critique of the idea that philosophy "has a monopoly on meaning and intelligibility" (Westphal 2008, p. 59). To make this point, Levinas stages a distinction between the God of the Bible—whom he positions as a God who transcends philosophical thought—and the God of the philosophers. While philosophy, for example in the form of what Levinas calls "rational theology," tries to capture the meaning of God by pulling God into the domain of being—thus denying and even destroying the very possibility of transcendence (see Levinas 1998a, p. 56)—Levinas tries to keep a place for a meaning "beyond being" (ibid., p. 57). This does *not* require that philosophy bring the idea of transcendence within its thought—because by doing that, transcendence would be pulled back into a confined domain of meaning-as-being—but rather requires that philosophy be transcended, that it is interrupted, that its fundamental *in*completeness is exposed. Philosophy might try to open itself for such an interruption, although there cannot be any guarantee of success, of course, as an interruption that really interrupts always arrives unexpected, as a thief in the night. Philosophy might also deny the need for transcendence and shield itself off for any possible interruption, thus trying to maintain its self-chosen self-sufficiency. While philosophy might perhaps be forgiven for such a strategy, I do not think that this is a viable option for philosophy *of education*—if, that is, philosophy of education does not wish to collapse into a philosophy of learning in which teaching has no place. As I have discussed in Chapter 1, the educational interest is, after all, an interest in the coming into the world of what is uniquely and radically new, which means that philosophy of education must always make place for that which cannot be foreseen as a possibility, that which transcends the realm of the possible.

RECEIVING THE GIFT OF TEACHING

The argument so far suggests that if teaching is to have a meaning *beyond* the facilitation of learning, if it is *essential* rather than *accidental* to learning, then it has to come with a notion of "transcendence." It has to be understood as something that comes from the *outside* and brings something *radically new*. This is what we can find in Climacus's idea of teaching as "double truth giving," and in Levinas's understanding of teaching as a relationship in which I receive from the other "beyond the capacity of the I." It is important to note, however, that both Climacus and Levinas are not so much saying that teaching *is* possible; they are rather inquiring into the *meaning* of teaching and into its conditions. Climacus is actually rather quick to assert that when we move from the *hypothetical* question as to what would have to be true "*if* the teacher were really to teach so that the relation to the teacher would be essential rather than accidental" (Westphal 2008, p. 25) to the question whether the teacher is *actually* capable of double truth giving, that this capacity lies *beyond* the powers of the teacher. He explicitly states that "the one who not only gives the learner the truth but provides the condition [for understanding it as truth] is not a teacher" (Kierkegaard 1985, p. 14). While Climacus acknowledges that "all instruction depends on the presence of the condition [so that] if it is lacking, a teacher is capable of nothing" (ibid.), he argues that "no human being" is capable of transforming the learner in such a way that the learner comes in the possession of the condition for understanding the truth as truth (ibid.). If such a transformation is to take place, Climacus therefore concludes, "it must be done by the god himself" (ibid., p. 15).

While Climacus approaches the question of teaching from the perspective of the teacher—and thus comes to the conclusion that the double truth giving that characterizes teaching is a gift that lies beyond the capacity of the teacher—Levinas engages with the question of teaching from the other end of the spectrum, that is, from the perspective of the one who is receiving from the other "beyond the capacity of the I." As I have mentioned, Levinas characterizes this experience as the experience of "being taught." The language is of crucial importance here because, so I wish to suggest, the experience of "being taught by" is radically different from the experience of "learning from." When students *learn from* their teacher, we could say that they use their teachers as a resource, just like a book or like the Internet. Moreover, when they learn from their teachers, they bring their teachers and what their teachers do or say within their own circle of understanding, within their own construction. This means that they are basically in control of what they learn from their teachers.

My point here is not to suggest that there is no place for such learning from teachers—although it does raise the question why in that situation we would still use the word *teacher* and not, for example, a word such as *resource*. My point rather is that *to learn from someone is a radically different experience from the experience of being taught by someone.* When we think, just at the level of "everyday phenomenology," of experiences where we were taught something—where we would say, always in hindsight, that "this person has really taught me something"—we more often than not refer to experiences where someone showed us something or made us realize something *that really entered our being from the outside.* Such teachings often provide insights about ourselves and our ways of doing and being—insights that we were not aware of or rather did not want to be aware of. They are inconvenient truths or, in the words of Deborah Britzman, cases of "difficult knowledge" (Britzman 1998).

While Levinas appears to be less radical than Climacus in that, unlike Climacus, he considers it possible that we *can* be taught by our teachers, the juxtaposition of Climacus and Levinas is nonetheless important as it helps to make clear that the experience of being taught, the experience of receiving the gift of teaching, is not an experience that can be *produced* by the teacher—which means that the teacher's power to teach is a weak, existential power, a power that relies on interaction and encounter and not a strong, metaphysical power. In precisely this sense Derrida's observation that to give a gift "is to give something that you don't have" (Derrida, quoted in Caputo and Vattimo 2007, p. 135) is entirely correct where it concerns the gift of teaching. Whether someone will be taught by what the teacher teaches lies beyond the control and power of the teacher (see also Saeverot 2011), which doesn't mean, though, that it doesn't matter what the teacher does (see below). Looking at teaching and being taught in this way, we might even say that in this precise sense the identity of the teacher has to be understood as a *sporadic* identity, an identity that only emerges at those moments when the gift of teaching is received. It is not an identity that can be claimed by the teacher; it is not an identity that can be in the teacher's secure possession. It rather is a possibility to reckon with, a possibility to work with in our lives as teachers. Calling someone a teacher is therefore ultimately not a matter of referring to a job title or a profession, but is a kind of compliment we pay when we acknowledge—and when we are able to acknowledge—that someone has indeed taught us something, that someone has indeed revealed something to us and that therefore we have been taught.[4]

Is teaching thus understood still a matter of truth giving? I believe it is *if,* that is, we understand the truth that is given, the truth that is offered to us, *not* as objective truth but as what Kierkegaard calls subjective or existential truth (see Kierkegaard 1992). Subjective truth as the "truth that is true for me," the truth "for which I am willing to live and die" (Kierkegaard 1996, p. 32), is to be understood as the truth that I have managed to give a place in my life, the truth that I have managed to receive, even more so if this truth is a difficult or inconvenient truth and, in that sense, an unwelcome truth. The difference between objective truth and subjective truth, then, is the difference between a set of propositions that I assert to be true—and here "what is reflected upon is not the relation [between the knower and the truth] but that what [the knower] relates himself to" (Kierkegaard 1992, p. 199)—and a truth I have managed to give a place in my existence—so that what matters is "the individual's relation" (ibid.) to the truth. This is about *how* the individual relates to the truth, as Climacus puts it, rather than *what* the individual relates to. The difference between objective truth and subjective truth, therefore, does not coincide with the difference between truth and falsehood or between objectivism and relativism, but has to do with the distinction between the theoretical and the existential, that is, between *what is true* and *what matters.* Since in the theoretical plane we can always ask further ques-

---

4. I would like to thank Jeroen Lutters for this insight. Note that to pay this compliment is not meant as a return of the gift of teaching; it is not a "payback"—see also note 5 below.

tions, we can always discover that what was considered to be objectively true turns out to be not so—which is how we can understand the ongoing "quest for certainty" that is called "science"—subjective truth is a relation neither to objective truth nor to relative truth but to what Climacus characterizes as "an objective uncertainty" (ibid., p. 203).

Caputo (2007, pp. 61–62) explains the difference as follows:

> In objective truth, the accent falls on the objective contact of what you say (which Climacus calls the "what"), so that if you get the objective content right (2 + 3 = 5) you are in the truth, no matter whether you are, in your personal subjectivity, a villain or an apostle. Nothing prevents a famous mathematician from being an ethical scoundrel. The existential subject is accidental and remains a disinterested spectator. But in subjective—or "existential" truth, the accent falls on what Climacus calls the "how," on the way the subject lives, the real life and "existence" of the subject. Here, where "subjectivity is truth," the subject is essential and passionately involved. In this case, even if what is said is objectively true—that God is love—if you are not subjectively transformed by that, if you do not personally have love in your heart, then you do not have the truth.... The difference is between having an idea of the "true God" and having a "true *relationship to* God." Here the how of the relationship is all. (Emphasis in original)

Looking at the experience of being taught in this way also makes it possible to give the idea of authority (again) a place in our understanding of teaching. The events of 1968 have clearly shown what the problem is with authority that is authoritarian, that is, authority that is nothing but the unwarranted exercise of power. Such authority is actually unable to work educationally, as it operates on a denial of the subjectivity of those who are subjected to such authority. But just as authoritarian education is and ought to be an oxymoron, so is anti-authoritarian education, that is, education that, in the words of A. S. Neil (1966), conflates freedom with license, and assumes that the promotion of freedom means that anything should go. As I have hinted at in the Prologue, the educational question—unlike the learning question—is not about doing what you want to do but requires engagement with the difference between what is *desired* and what is *desirable*. The educational question, in other words, is about what it is that we want to give authority to; it is about deciding what it is that we want to have authority in our lives. To receive the gift of teaching, to welcome the unwelcome, to give a place to inconvenient truths and difficult knowledge, is precisely the moment where we *give authority* to the teaching we receive. In this sense—and presumably only in this sense—can the idea of authority have a meaningful place in education (see also Meirieu 2007; Bingham 2009).[5]

CONCLUSIONS

This chapter has been motivated by a very concrete and practical concern about the disappearance of teaching and the demise of the role of the teacher as someone who has something to say and something to bring. This, as I have shown, is not merely a theoretical or philosophical discussion but is having a real impact on common perceptions about teaching and even on the self-perception of teachers. In response to this I have argued that if teaching is to be more than just the facilitation of learning or the creation of learning environments, it needs to carry with it an idea of transcendence. I have not only tried to make clear what "kind" of transcendence is needed. I have also tried to indicate what it means to think transcendence consistently, which, as I have suggested, is not merely a matter of thought or comprehension but also entails taking the idea and possibility of revelation seriously, as both a religious and a secular concept. In doing this I have tried to suggest that transcendence cannot be contained to the other as another human being. As soon as one brings transcendence in, one has to take it seriously all the way down—or perhaps we should say all the way "up."

While this does suggest that the idea of teaching, if it is to have any meaning beyond the facilitation of learning, needs to come with a notion of "transcendence," it does not mean that the teacher can simply and unproblem-atically occupy such a position of transcendence. (As I have highlighted, the power to teach is the very thing that is not in the possession of the teacher.) One reason for this lies in the fact that teachers can never fully control the "impact" of their activities on their students. In this regard—and here lies a connection to the discussion of the theme of "communication" in the previous chapter—the educational "project" always needs to engage with its own impossibility (see Vanderstraeten and Biesta 2001; Biesta 2004a; Green 2010; Gough 2010) and thus needs to proceed with a sense of irony, that is, with a sense of disbelief in itself, a sense of powerlessness or weakness. The other, perhaps more important reason has to do with the fact that claiming a

---

5. It is important to note that to give authority to the teaching we receive should not be understood as the point where we "return" the gift of teaching, where we pay for what is given to us, so as to annul the gift and turn it into an economy (see Derrida 1992b).

position of transcendence runs the risk of turning educational authority into educational authoritarianism, which would block the very education one aims to bring about.

This is why I have approached the question of teaching from the perspective of the experience of "being taught," which, as I have emphasized, is fundamentally different from the experience of "learning from." While in the situation where students learn from their teachers, the teacher figures as a resource so that what is being learned from the teacher is within the control of the student, the experience of "being taught" is about those situations in which something enters our being from the outside, so to speak, as something that is fundamentally beyond the control of the "learner." To be taught—to be open to receiving the gift of teaching—thus means being able to give such interruptions a place in one's understanding and one's being. This is why, following Kierkegaard, such teachings, when they are received, are a matter of subjective truth, that is, of truth to which we are willing to give authority.

Does the fact that teachers cannot produce the experience of "being taught" mean that teachers can do nothing in this domain other than hope for the best? I do not think that this is the conclusion that necessarily follows. One thing that teachers and those who have a concern for teaching can do is to resist and interrupt the constructivist "common sense" about teaching (see also Chapter 4)—a "common sense" in which the teacher is the one who has nothing to give and is giving nothing, who is there to draw out what is already inside the student, who is there to facilitate students' learning rather than to teach them a lesson, who is there to make the learning process as smooth and enjoyable as possible, who will not ask difficult questions or introduce difficult knowledge, in the hope that students will leave as satisfied customers. There is, after all, a different story to tell about teaching, and it is important that this story is being told and enacted—both within the school and within society. This is a story where teachers are not disposable and dispensable resources for learning, but where they have something to give, where they do not shy away from difficult questions and inconvenient truths, and where they work actively and consistently on the distinction between what is *desired* and what is *desirable,* so as to explore what it is that should have authority in our lives. And this is not only a question at the level of individual students and their desires, but also has to do with the public role of the teacher (see Meirieu 2008), so as to (re)connect the project of schooling with the wider democratic transformation of individual "wants" into collectively agreed upon "needs" (see Heller and Fehér 1989; Biesta 2011b).

Just as there is a need to tell and enact a different story about teaching and the teacher, there is also a need to tell and enact a different story about the student, a story where the student is not a student-consumer whose needs need to be met in the most effective way, but a student who is open to the gift of teaching, a student who can welcome the unwelcome, a student who does not limit himself or herself to the task of learning from the teacher but is open to the possibility of being taught. To open oneself for such a possibility begins, perhaps, by acknowledging that the school is not and should not be understood as a place for *learning*—if one wishes one can, after all, learn anywhere—but that what makes the school a school is the fact that it is a place for *teaching,* as this is what is distinctive about the school compared to most if not all social institutions, settings, and arrangements. To enter the school on the assumption that one may not only learn but perhaps even be taught may only be a very small shift, but it is nonetheless a crucial and necessary shift if our aim is to give teaching its proper place in education or, to put it differently, if our aim is to give teaching back to education.

CHAPTER FOUR

Learning

To live, by definition, is not something one learns.

—*Jacques Derrida*

So far I have discussed three educational themes—creativity, communication, and teaching—and in each case I have highlighted weak dimensions and elements in order to show that such dimensions are not *accidental*—they are not a defect, to put it differently—but that they are *essential* to what it means to create, to communicate, and to teach. To create, to communicate, and to teach are thus not to be understood as processes that can be controlled by the creator, the communicator, or the teacher. Precisely in this sense they always entail a risk. Engaging with this risk—and perhaps we could even say, embracing the risk—is what makes such processes educationally relevant and significant. It gives them an educational "force," albeit not a strong metaphysical force but rather a weak existential force. In this chapter I turn to the theme of learning. While some people would see this as the central theme in any discussion about education, I have, over the years, become increasingly concerned about the language and discourse of learning (see Biesta 2006a, 2010b; see also below). In my more radical moments I sometimes even think that learning is the last thing that educators should be concerned about—and the distinction between "learning from" and "being taught by" that I introduced in the previous chapter provides perhaps some reason for this suggestion.

In this chapter I therefore come to the theme of learning from a rather critical angle. The main "target" for my critique is the suggestion that learning is something natural, something we cannot *not* do. Against the idea that learning is something natural, I argue that learning is something constructed—that when we refer to something as "learning" we are not engaged in a description of a naturally occurring phenomenon but are actually making a judgment about change. Such judgments are important in educational settings—which is one of the reasons why, as I will explain below and have argued before, the language of learning is unhelpful as an educational language—and it is important to see them for what they are, that is, normative judgments about desirable change, not descriptions of inevitable natural processes. To see learning as something constructed and artificial makes it possible to expose the political "work" done through the idea of "learning," something I will explore in more detail in terms of what I will refer to as the "politics of learning." Against the background of an analysis of the politics of learning that is at work in contemporary discussions about lifelong learning, I show how the idea of learning as something natural, something we cannot *not* do, runs the risk of keeping people in their place. This is why in the later parts of the chapter I turn to the theme of emancipation in order to explore whether it is possible to think of emancipation outside of the confines of a certain politics of learning. With Foucault I explore the emancipatory potential of the ideas of resistance, interruption, and transgression in order to highlight the need for resisting the idea of the learner identity as a natural and inevitable identity and for interrupting the current "common sense" about learning.

My attempt to denaturalize the idea of learning—that is, to take it out of the domain of inevitability and necessity—can be understood as an attempt to take the strength out of the idea of learning, not only in order to show that it is a more complicated and contentious notion than many would believe but also to show that learning is not something that has power over us—something to which we should subject ourselves—but rather something that *we* should have power over. To take the strength out of the idea of learning is therefore another contribution to the exploration of the weak dimensions of education.

Learning, Learning, Learning

In the preamble to his book *Specters of Marx,* Jacques Derrida writes that "to live, by definition, is not something one learns" (Derrida 1994, p. xviii). If this is indeed so, and if it is so *by definition,* then the following lines, taken from the preface of UNESCO's report from the *2010 Shanghai International Forum on Lifelong Learning,* may perhaps sound a little "out of joint." They read,

> We are now living in a fast-changing and complex social, economic and political world to which we need to adapt by increasingly rapidly acquiring

new knowledge, skills and attitudes in a wide range of contexts. An individual will not be able to meet life challenges unless he or she becomes a lifelong learner, and a society will not be sustainable unless it becomes a learning society. (Yang and Valdés-Cotera 2011, p. v)

Claims like these—which almost sound like threats: You will not be able to meet life challenges unless you become a lifelong learner! Society will not be sustainable unless it becomes a learning society!—have become all too familiar in recent times, so that it may well be argued that we now live in a "learning age" (which incidentally was the title of a UK government consultation paper from 1998 that even promised "a renaissance for a new Britain"—see Department for Education and Employment 1998).

In the learning age we are surrounded by claims that learning is something good and desirable, and often by claims that it is *intrinsically* good and desirable. We are also surrounded by claims that learning is something inevitable, something we *have* to do and cannot *not* do, and therefore as something that should not only take place in schools, colleges, and universities but actually should go on throughout our lives, both extended in time (the idea of life*long* learning) and extended in space (the idea of life-*wide* learning, that is, learning that permeates all aspects of our lives). But is learning indeed "the treasure within"—as was suggested in the title of the 1996 UNESCO report written by Jacques Delors and colleagues (Delors et al. 1996)? Is learning indeed inevitable? Is it indeed an "unavoidable biological fact [that] we learn as we breathe, all the time, without giving it any thought" (Field 2000, p. 35)? Is learning therefore indeed something that *should* permeate our lives, from dusk to dawn, from cradle to grave, from womb to tomb? And is it therefore entirely reasonable to have European Lifelong Learning Indicators that measure in extreme detail how "well" each and every European country and within each country ultimately every individual is doing in its learning (see ELLI Development Team 2008)?

In this chapter I raise a number of critical questions about the "learning age," that is, about the apparent omnipresence of learning in our times and our lives. These questions partly have to do with *discourse,* that is, with the discourse of learning and its problems. They partly have to do with *power,* that is, with the ways in which through the discourse of learning power is being exercised. And they have to do with *resistance,* that is, with the question whether we should resist the "demand" for learning and, if so, how we might be able to do this. I come to these questions as an educator and educationalist, as I think that the language of learning has been utterly unhelpful in the double educational task of engagement with and emancipation from the world, both the material and the social world (on this formulation of the "task" of educa-tion see, for example, Meirieu 2007). The analytical and critical "device" I will use in this chapter is the idea of the "politics of learning," through which I will highlight the powerful work that is being done by and at the very same time hidden behind the discourse of "learning." I will develop my ideas in five steps. I will start with the discourse of learning, indicating, on the one hand, the ongoing "learnification" of the discourse of education and highlighting, on the other hand, some problems with the very idea of "learning." Against this background I then look at shifts in the "field" of lifelong learning (and here we should note that to name this "field" in terms of learning is already part of the problem) in order to explore some aspects of a politics of learning that is working through it. I will then make some suggestions for how we might resist the tendency to naturalize learning—that is, to put it on an equal footing with breathing and digestion—both at the level of theory and the level of practice. From there I turn to the question of emancipation in order to explore how we might think of and "do" emancipation outside of the confines of a politics of learning. What such an emancipation-without-learning might look like is something that, in the fifth step, I illustrate through the work of Foucault. After this I will make some concluding remarks to draw the lines of my argument together.

THE PROBLEM WITH "LEARNING"

Since the 1990s the word *learning* has become a popular concept in educational research, policy, and practice. Elsewhere (Biesta 2010b) I have characterized the rapid increase in the use of the word *learning* and the rise of a wider "language of learning" as the *learnification* of educational discourse and practice. This process is visible in a number of discursive shifts, such as the tendency to refer to education as "teaching and learning," to refer to students as "learners" and to adults as "adult learners," to see teachers as "facilitators of learning," and to conceive of schools as "learning environments" or "places for learning"—the latter being the phrase used to designate Watercliffe Meadow, a primary school in Sheffield, allegedly because the word *school* had such a negative connotation with pupils and parents.[1] The shift from "adult education" to "lifelong learn-ing" is another prominent manifestation of the rise of this "new language of learning" (Biesta 2006a).

---

1. See http://en.wikipedia.org/wiki/Watercliffe_Meadow (last accessed August 15, 2012).

The rise of the "new language of learning" is the result—and perhaps we should say the partly unintended outcome—of a number of developments. These include (1) the impact of new theories of learning, particularly constructivist theories, that put the focus more strongly on students and their activities than on teachers and their input; (2) the (postmodern) critique of authoritarian forms of teaching; (3) what John Field (2000) has called the "silent explosion" of learning, that is, the fact that more and more people are engaged in more and more different forms and modes of learning, particularly nonformal and informal ones; and (4) the individualizing impact of neoliberal policies and politics on education, including adult education (a point to which I will return). The rise of the language of learning has, in some cases, empowered those at the receiving end of the spectrum, particularly where teaching was conceived in narrow, controlling, and authoritarian ways. But the rise of a language of learning has also had some less desirable consequences. These consequences have to do with two aspects of the concept of "learning," one being that "learning" is a process term, and the other that "learning," unlike "education," is an individualistic and individualizing term.

To begin with the first point: in the English language "learning" generally denotes a process or an activity. This means, however, that the word *learning* is in itself neutral or empty with regard to content, direction, and purpose. To suggest that learning is good or desirable—and thus to suggest that it is something that should go on throughout one's life or that should be promoted in schools—does therefore not really mean anything until it is specified what the *content* of the learning is and, more important, until it is specified what the *purpose* of the learning is. This emptiness of the notion of "learning" has made its rise in educational settings quite problematic, as the point of education—be it school education or the education of adults—is never just that students learn, but that they learn *something* and that they learn this for particular *reasons.* The language of learning has made it far more difficult to engage with the question of purpose to the extent that in many instances this question has virtually disappeared from the discussion (see Biesta 2010b). The fact that "learning" is an individualistic and individualizing term—learning is, after all, something one can only do for oneself; it is not possible to learn for somebody else—has also shifted attention away from the importance of *relationships* in educational processes and practices and has thus made it far more difficult to explore what the particular responsibilities and tasks of educational professionals such as teachers and adult educators actually are.

As soon as it is acknowledged that the question of learning always raises further questions about its purposes, we can, on the one hand, begin to ask what desirable purposes of learning might be, while, on the other hand, we can begin to see the particular purposes that are being promoted in policies and practices for lifelong learning. With regard to the first issue it has been known for a long time in the field of adult education that the learning of adults is not one-dimensional but can serve a range of different purposes. Aspin and Chapman (2001) helpfully make a distinction between three different agendas for lifelong learning: lifelong learning for economic progress and development; lifelong learning for personal development and fulfillment; and lifelong learning for social inclusiveness and democratic understanding and activity (see Aspin and Chapman 2001, pp. 39–40). As I have already mentioned earlier in this book, I have elsewhere (Biesta 2010b) proposed a distinction between three domains of educational purpose: the domain of *qualification,* which has to do with the ways in which, through education, individuals become qualified to do certain things (this is the domain of the acquisition of knowledge, skills, values, and dispositions); the domain of *socialization,* which has to do with the ways in which, through education, individuals become part of existing social, political, professional, and so on "orders"; and the domain of *subjectification,* which, in opposition to socialization, is not about how individuals become part of existing orders but how they can be independent—or as some would say, autonomous—subjects of action and responsibility. While qualification and socialization can contribute to the empowerment of individuals in that it gives them the power to operate within existing sociopolitical configurations and settings, subjectification has an orientation toward emancipation, that is, toward ways of doing and being that do not simply accept the given order but have an orientation toward the change of the existing order so that different ways of doing and being become possible. (I return to this below.)

The problem with the language of learning, therefore, is that it tends to obscure crucial dimensions of educational processes and practices—that is, aspects of content, purpose, and relationships. This means not only that the language of learning is a very unhelpful language in the field of education (and there is indeed evidence that this is impacting negatively on the ability of teachers to engage with the normative and political dimensions of their work; see, for example, Biesta 2010b, p. 4)—which is why I have coined the ugly word *learnification* to highlight this—but also that it is obscuring the political "work" that is done with and through the language of learning. To this issue I will now turn.

THE POLITICS OF LEARNING

While there are many examples of the learnification of educational discourse in the domain of school, college, and university education, the "field" where this has happened most explicitly and most extremely is that of lifelong learning. As I have indicated, the very fact that this field is now being called lifelong *learning* already highlights the impact of the language of learning on this domain. While the interest in the "lifelong" dimension has been around for a long time—for example, in the work of Basil Yeaxlee in Britain and Eduard Lindeman in the United States (both in the 1920s)—the idea of "lifelong" has for a long time been connected to the notion of *education* (the title of Yeaxlee's book from 1929 was indeed *Lifelong Education*) and not to that of *learning*. Even in the 1970s the rise of interest in the "lifelong" dimension was always connected to education, such as in the landmark 1972 UNESCO report *Learning to Be: The World of Education Today and Tomorrow* (Faure et al. 1972) or even in one of the early OECD contributions to the discussion, the 1973 report *Recurrent Education* (Organisation for Economic Co-operation and Development 1973).

Two decades later UNESCO was still pursuing the education line, for example in the 1996 report *Learning: The Treasure Within* (Delors et al. 1996)—but do note the title—which not only argued for the need "to rethink and broaden the notion of lifelong education" so that it not only focuses on adaptation "to changes in the nature of work" but also constitutes "a continuous process of forming whole human beings" (ibid., p. 19), but also argued for a shift in attention "from social cohesion to democratic participation" (ibid., chapter 2) and "from economic growth to human development" (ibid., chapter 3), paying explicit attention to the political, democratic, and global dimensions of lifelong learning. *Learning: The Treasure Within* can, in a sense, be read as a response to a rapidly emerging alternative discourse on lifelong learning, one strongly characterized by an economic rationale and a focus on lifelong learning as the development of human capital.

The idea that lifelong learning is first and foremost about the development of human capital so as to secure competitiveness and economic growth played a central role in an influential document published by the OECD in 1997, with the title *Lifelong Learning for All*. *Lifelong Learning for All* put a strong emphasis on the economic rationale for lifelong learning—itself understood in the rather formal sense as learning "throughout life" (Organisation for Economic Co-operation and Development 1997, p. 15). It presented the idea of "lifelong learning for all" as "the guiding principle for policy strategies that will respond directly to the need to improve the capacity of individuals, families, workplaces and communities to continuously adapt and renew" (ibid., p. 13). Such adaptation and renewal are presented as necessary in the face of changes in the global economy and the world of work. Lifelong learning "from early childhood education to active learning in retirement" is thus presented as "an important factor in promoting employment and economic development" and, in addition to this, also in promoting "democracy and social cohesion" (ibid., p. 13). Whereas, as mentioned, the Delors report made a case for shifting the attention from social cohesion *to* democratic participation and from economic growth to human development, *Lifelong Learning for All* went in the opposite direction where it concerns economic growth, seeing democracy and social cohesion as compatible agendas rather than as agendas that are potentially in tension with each other (on this see also Biesta 2006c).

The shift from lifelong education to lifelong learning signifies a number of things. It is first of all a shift in orientation from lifelong education having to do with personal and democratic aims toward an economic if not *economistic*[2] rationale, in which lifelong learning becomes a matter of the abstract production of human capital, both at the level of individuals and their skills and competences and at the more macro-level where lifelong learning then appears as "a key strategy to adjust human capital to new requirements" (ELLI Development Team 2008, p. 8). It is, however, not only the *orientation* of lifelong learning that has changed; there are also important changes with regard to its *form*. One significant change is the ongoing *individualization* of lifelong learning, something that Field (2000) shows empirically—his idea of a silent explosion—but that can also be found ideologically, for example in the emphasis on the need for individuals to adapt and adjust to the demands of the global economy, in the reformulation of lifelong learning as the acquisition of a set of flexible skills and competencies, and also, of course, in the subtle but crucial semantic shift from "lifelong education"—a *relational* concept—to "lifelong learning"—an *individualistic* concept.

While this is a matter of "form," it is also a matter of politics. The most important shift at this level concerns the transformation of lifelong learning as a *right* that individuals can claim into a *duty* that all individuals need to live up to (as a more careful reading of the title of the OECD's 1997 *Lifelong Learning for All* can reveal: not lifelong learning as *available to* all but lifelong learning as *demanded from* all). Messerschmidt (2011, p. 18) has connected this shift—which she characterizes as the emergence of a kind of

---

2. I use "economistic" here as referring to the idea of the economy as an aim and value in itself—similar to the difference between "scientific" and "scientistic."

"Bildungspflicht" (a duty to education)—to the Lisbon Strategy[3] and highlights, correctly in my view, that with the rise of the duty to "Bildung," one of the key characteristics of adult education, namely, the voluntary nature of participation, has disappeared.

Elsewhere (Biesta 2006c, pp. 175–176) I have argued that we can also see this shift as a *reversal* of rights and duties in that under the lifelong *education* paradigm, individuals had a right to lifelong education and the state a duty to provide resources and opportunities, whereas under the lifelong *learning* paradigm, individuals have ended up with the duty to learn throughout life, whereas the state now seems to be in a position where it can claim the right to demand of all its citizens that they learn throughout their lives. One telling example of this is the rise of the notion of "hard-to-reach-learners" in lifelong learning policy in the United Kingdom and in other English-speaking countries (see, for example, Brackertz 2007), suggesting that somewhere in the dark concerns of society there are still a few individuals who refuse to live up to their learning duty.

It is here that we can begin to see the politics of learning at work. There are a number of aspects to this. One key dimension of the politics of learning is the increasing tendency to turn politic problems into learning problems, thus shifting the responsibility for addressing such problems from the state and the collective to the level of individuals. We can see this clearly in the rise of the economic rationale and the fact that individuals are made responsible for keeping up their employability in rapidly changing global markets, rather than that the question is raised why such markets should rule over the economy and over social and political life more generally in the first place. The issue is entirely defined as a question of individual *adaptation and adjustment*—as a matter of learning—and not as one about structural issues and collective responsibilities.

The pressure is, however, coming not only from the outside but also from the inside. This has to do with the very "construction" of the lifelong learner identity as a process of Foucauldian "governmentality," where individuals begin to identify with and then internalize the demand for lifelong

---

3. The Lisbon Strategy is the name for an action-and-development plan initiated in 2000 with the aim to make the European Union the most competitive and dynamic knowledge-based economy in the world, capable of sustainable economic growth with more and better jobs and greater social cohesion. It has had a significant impact on education in the member countries also through the so-called Bologna Process, aimed at the harmonization of higher education across the EU member states.

learning. They thus do not simply become "permanently learning subjects" (Field 2000, p. 35) as a result of external pressures, but actually feel an internal "need" to construct and conduct themselves in this way (see, for example, Forneck and Wrana 2005; Fejes 2006; Biesta 2006c). Rather than a "treasure within," learning thus turns into a "pressure within," so that the politics of learning is being fed by our apparent will to learn (see Simons and Masschelein 2009).

The politics of learning is also at work in the shift from a democratic interest in lifelong education and lifelong learning toward an emphasis on social cohesion and integration. Part of the problem here—a simple but crucial one—is that a cohesive society is not necessarily or automatically also a democratic society. Also, notions of social integration and cohesion always raise the question as to who needs to be integrated into what or cohere with whom, and also who is allowed to set the agenda and define the terms of integration and cohesion (see also Biesta 2010b, chapter 6). And again lifelong learning is being mobilized to facilitate integration and cohesion through processes of adaptation and adjustment similar to what we have seen with regard to adaptation and adjustment to the "demands" of the economy.

The fourth aspect of the politics of learning that I wish to highlight has to do with the *naturalization* of learning, that is, with the tendency to see learning as an entirely natural phenomenon—on the same par as breathing and digestion. To suggest that learning is simply part of our biological and increasingly also our neurological "makeup" and therefore as something we cannot help but do—something we cannot *not* do—leads to a slippery slope where (1) learning first becomes equated with living, (2) then almost necessarily becomes a lifelong process, which (3) next moves to the claim that any normal human being *can* learn, (4) then easily moves to the suggestion that therefore every normal human being *should* learn, so that (5) in the end, there must be something wrong with you if you do not want to learn and refuse the learner identity.

To highlight these aspects of the politics of learning—that is, the political work that is being done through the notion and language and discourse of learning—is not to deny that there may be some good aspects to learning (although I am becoming less and less optimistic about this precisely because of the problems outlined above), but to be aware that the language of learning is not an innocent language but actually a language that exerts a powerful influence on what we can be and how we can be, one that tends to domesticate rather than to emancipate. But if this is so, what are the opportunities for resistance, and what might learning still have to do there? Let me now turn to these questions.

DENATURALIZING LEARNING IS REPOLITICIZING LEARNING, REPOLITICIZING LEARNING REQUIRES DENATURALIZING LEARNING

If part of the way in which the politics of learning is able to do its work stems from the suggestion that learning is a natural process and phenomenon, then the first step toward exposing the political work being done through learning is by denaturalizing learning, that is, highlighting what we might call the artificial nature of learning. One way to denaturalize the idea of learning is by acknowledging that "learning" is an *evaluative* concept, not a descriptive one. If we start from the widely accepted definition of learning as any more or less durable change that is not the result of maturation, we can see that when we use the word *learning*—for example, in such sentences as "John has learned to ride a bicycle" or "Mary has learned the first law of thermodynamics"—we are not so much *describing* change as that we are making a *judgment* about change. The point is that when we observe John more carefully we will probably be able to identify numerous things that have changed. The reason for identifying some of these changes as "learning" and others as "just changes" is because we *value* these changes—either positively, for example, when we are proud that John has learned to ride his bike, or negatively, for example, when John has picked up some bad habits in the process—and because we have reason to believe that, at least to a certain extent, these changes are the result of interaction with an environment and not just the outcome of maturation.

This indicates that "learning" expresses a *judgment,* which suggests that when we use the word *learning* we are not so much describing a fact as that we are evaluating an event. (We could say, therefore, that learning is not a noun.) It is this judgment, then, that constitutes change as learning. To see "learning" as an evaluative term can be an effective way to denaturalize the idea of learning because it allows us, each time the word *learning* is being used, not only to ask what kind of judgment is being made—that is, what the reasons are for identifying particular change as learning—but also to ask who is involved in making the judgment; who, in other words, claims the power to define particular change as learning (and other change "just" as change).

The other way in which the idea of learning can be denaturalized is by simply refusing the very identity of a learner, thus showing that this identity is not inevitable but *can* actually be refused (see also Simons and Masschelein 2009). Such a refusal can help to make visible that calling someone a learner is actually a very specific intervention, where the claim is made that the one who is being called a learner lacks something, is not yet complete or competent, and therefore needs to engage in further "learning activity." While in some specific cases it is entirely legitimate to make this assumption—for example, if one has an explicit desire to master a particular skill or gain particular knowledge or understanding—it is important to keep the learner identity confined to such cases and see it as a pragmatic, time-bound, and situation-bound *choice*, and not as a natural state of affairs. Moreover, in some cases it can actually be politically important to refuse the learner identity, particularly in those cases where, as mentioned above, the learner identity is being used to burden individuals with tasks, demands, and duties that should be the responsibility of the collective. To refuse the learner identity, to claim that in some cases there is actually nothing to learn—for example, to claim that one can speak as a citizen without first having to learn what it means to speak "properly" (see below; see also Biesta 2011b)—is not to denounce the importance of learning, but to denaturalize and hence politicize learning so that choices, politics, and power become visible. To refuse the learner identity thus at the very same time *exposes* and *opposes* the politics of learning at work.

Emancipation without Learning?

If the ideas presented so far make some sense, I would, in the final step of this chapter, like to connect this to the difficult but important issue of emancipation. After all, if it is the case that learning has to a large extent become an instrument of domestication if not, to use the beautiful word for which we have to thank the translator of Rancière (see Rancière 1991a), an instrument of stultification, then the important question for (us) educators is whether we can still envisage opportunities for emancipation and, more specifically, for emancipation without learning. There are two authors who in my view have made important contributions to this challenge—one being Michel Foucault, the other being Jacques Rancière. In the remainder of this chapter I will confine myself to presenting Foucault's ideas as an example of an understanding of emancipation-without-learning. I turn to Rancière in Chapter 5. Let me, in this section, say something about the role learning plays in "modern" understandings of emancipation in order then, in the next section, to see whether, with Foucault, we can envisage emancipation *without* learning.

The idea that emancipation requires learning is one that partly has come to us from the Enlightenment and Immanuel Kant's suggestion that we can escape or overcome our immaturity—our determination by the other—if we have the courage to make use of our rational capacities. But more explicitly the connection between emancipation and learning can be found in the Marxist idea that in order to liberate ourselves from the oppressive workings of power, we need to expose how power operates. A central idea here that, in turn, has strongly influenced critical and emancipatory pedagogies, is the notion of ideology, which not only expresses the claim that all thought is socially determined but also that ideological thought is thought that *denies* this determination. The "predicament of ideology" lies in the suggestion that it is precisely because of the way in which power works upon our consciousness, that we are unable to see how power works upon our consciousness. (I discuss this in more detail in the next chapter.) This not only implies that in order to free ourselves from the workings of power we need to expose how power works upon our consciousness. It also means that in order for us to achieve emancipation, *someone else,* whose consciousness is not subjected to the workings of power, needs to provide us with an account of our objective condition. According to this line of thought, therefore, emancipation is ultimately contingent upon the truth about our objective condition, a truth that can only be generated by someone who is positioned outside of the influence of ideology.

The educational "translation" of this "logic" of emancipation basically takes two forms, one that can be characterized as *monological* and one that can be characterized as *dialogical.* The monological approach is the most direct translation of the ideas outlined above. It relies on the assumption that emancipation requires an intervention from the outside—an intervention, moreover, by someone who is not subjected to the power that needs to be overcome. Thus emancipation appears as something that is *done to* somebody and hence relies on a fundamental *inequality* between the emancipator and the one to be emancipated. Equality, on this account, becomes the outcome of emancipation; it becomes something that lies in the future. Moreover, it is this outcome that is used to legitimize the interventions of the emancipator. This is a "logic" of emancipatory education—a logic that we might also call "colonial" (see, for example, Andreotti 2011)—in which the teacher knows and students do not know *yet*; where it is the task of the teacher to explain the world to the students and where it is the task of the students to ultimately become as knowledgeable as the teacher. In this setup there is a clear learning task for the student, a task that is basically *reproductive* in that it is aimed at the acquisition of the insights and understandings of the teacher-emancipator.

It is one of the main achievements of Paulo Freire to have provided a dialogical alternative in which emancipation is no longer seen as a process of truth-telling by the teacher-emancipator—Freire's notion of "banking education"—but where it becomes a process of the collective discovery of oppressive structures, processes, and practices, a process in which teacher and students are positioned as "co-subjects" (Freire 1972, p. 135). Freire characterizes oppression as the situation in which individuals are disconnected from the world and exist as objects of the oppressor's actions rather than as subjects of their own actions. Oppression is thus understood as a process of "dehumanization" that occurs when people's natural ways of "being-in-praxis" are disrupted or suppressed (ibid.). Emancipation on this account is aimed at restoring the connection between human beings and the world, or, in Freire's vocabulary, restoring *praxis*. The role of the teacher in this process is to reinstigate dialogical and reflective practices that in turn reinitiate praxis and link people back to the world (ibid., p. 30). For Freire emancipation therefore also involves learning—and more, perhaps, than in the banking model of emancipation, this is an ongoing and in a sense lifelong process. The learning is, however, not reproductive but constructive or generative, albeit that it still has an orientation toward truth. Unlike in the monological model, however, this is *not* the truth given by the teacher to students about their objective condition on the assumption that students are unable to acquire such insights themselves.

FOR EXAMPLE: FOUCAULT AND THE PRACTICE OF TRANSGRESSION

Although I have shown that truth occupies a different position in the monological and the dialogical approach, both approaches ultimately rely on the possibility of truth and, more specifically, truth uncontaminated by power. In the monological approach this truth is learned from the teacher; in the dialogical approach this truth is discovered through a collective learning process. That both approaches rely on the idea of truth uncontaminated by power has, in the monological approach, to do with the fact that emancipation is seen as a process of overcoming ideological distortions. Here emancipation operates as a process of *demystification*. In the dialogical approach emancipation is the process that restores true human existence—or in Freirean language, true human praxis. In both cases, truth is needed to overcome alienation, either the alienation produced by false consciousness or the alienation brought about by oppression. For truth to be able to do this "work," it must be assumed that there is a fundamental distinction between truth and power—and one could indeed argue that this distinction is foundational for the modern project of Enlightenment (for example, Habermas 1990), evidence of which we can find in the idea of "speaking truth to power."

One author who has challenged this very assumption is Michel Foucault. He has argued that power and knowledge *never* occur separately but always come together, something that is expressed in the idea of "power/knowledge."

This is why he has suggested that we should abandon "the whole tradition that allows us to imagine that knowledge can only exist where the power relations are suspended" (Foucault 1975, p. 27)—a tradition that forms the basis for both monological and dialogical approaches to emancipation. Yet to argue that we have to abandon this particular tradition is not to suggest that change is no longer possible. It rather is to highlight that we are always operating *within* power/knowledge "constellations"—that is, of power/knowledge *versus* power/knowledge—and not of knowledge versus power or power versus knowledge. There is, therefore, potential for action, change, and critique, but we have to understand this in terms that are fundamentally different from the idea that emancipation is an *escape* from power.[4]

Foucault agrees with Enlightenment thinkers such as Kant that criticism "consists of analyzing and reflecting upon limits" (Foucault 1984, p. 45). But "if the Kantian question was that of knowing what limits knowledge had to renounce transgressing, ... the critical question today has to be turned back into a positive one: in what is given to us as universal, necessary, obligatory, what place is occupied by whatever is singular, contingent, and the product of arbitrary constraints?" (ibid.). In some of his writings Foucault has referred to this approach as "eventalization" (Foucault 1991, p. 76). Eventalization "means making visible a singularity at places where there is a temptation to invoke a historical constant, an immediate anthropological trait, or an obviousness which imposes itself uniformly on all" (ibid.).[5] Eventalization works "by constructing around the singular event ... a 'polygon' or rather a 'polyhedron' of intelligibility, the number of whose faces is not given in advance and can never properly be taken as finite" (ibid., p. 77). Eventalization thus means to complicate and to pluralize our understanding of events, their elements, their relations, and their domains of reference.

Eventalization therefore does not result in a deeper understanding, an understanding of underlying structures or causes, and in this respect it does precisely *not* generate the kind of knowledge that will set us free from the workings of those structures or causes. But Foucault has been adamant that

---

4. My reading of Foucault differs from what I see as a very common misreading of Foucault that suggests he has given us ultimate knowledge about the operations of power. Such a reading still relies on the assumption that power and knowledge "operate" separately, yet it is precisely this assumption that has been challenged by Foucault. This doesn't mean that there is nothing to know about power, but it does mean that such knowledge is itself not "beyond" the workings of power.

5. What I have tried to do with the notion of "learning" in the earlier parts of this chapter can precisely be understood in this way.

this does not mean that such analysis is without effect. What eventalization does *not* generate, so he has argued, is advice or guidelines or instructions as to what is to be done. But what it can bring about is a situation in which people "'no longer know what they do,' so that the acts, gestures, discourses which up until then had seemed to go without saying become problematic, difficult, dangerous"—and this effect, so he argues, is entirely *intentional* (ibid., p. 84). Thus eventalization neither results in a deeper or truer understanding of how power works—it only tries to unsettle what is taken for granted—nor aims to produce recipes for action. This kind of analysis is therefore not meant to solve problems; it is not a kind of knowledge meant for "social workers" or "reformers" but rather for subjects who act. As Foucault explains,

> Critique doesn't have to be the premise of a deduction which concludes: this then is what needs to be done. It should be an instrument for those who fight, those who resist and refuse what is. Its use should be in processes of conflict and confrontation, essays in refusal. It doesn't have to lay down the law for the law. It isn't a stage of programming. It is a challenge directed to what is. (Ibid., p. 84)

Rather than to think of emancipation as an escape from power, Foucault envisages emancipation as a *"practical* critique that takes the form of a possible transgression" (Foucault 1984, p. 45; emphasis added). The critical practice of transgression is not meant to overcome limits (not in the least because limits are not only constraining but always also enabling; see Simons 1995, p. 69). Transgression rather is the practical and experimental "illumination of limits" (Foucault 1977, pp. 33–38; Boyne 1990)—such as in the attempt to see how far we can go in denying the very existence of learning or the very suggestion that learning has anything to do with us or that we have anything to do with learning.

Foucault's rejection of the founding distinction of modern Enlightenment—that is, the distinction between knowledge and power—does therefore not imply the end of the possibility of emancipation and the end of the possibility of critique, but makes emancipation from an endeavor based on truth—either the truth to be given by the teacher-emancipator or the truth discovered through collective critical learning—into the practical task of *transgression*. Transgression means doing things differently in order to show—or to prove, as Foucault would say—that things can be different and that the way things are is not the way things necessarily should be, for example, that we can also *not* be a lifelong learner. Thus the emancipatory potential of transgression lies in the possibility "of no longer being, doing, or thinking what we are, do, or think"—and in precisely this sense, Foucault suggests, "it is seeking to give a new impetus ... to the undefined work of freedom" (Foucault 1984, p. 46).

With Foucault we can thus begin to see the contours of a different understanding of and approach to emancipation, one where emancipation is no longer an escape from power through demystification but becomes a practice of transgression—the practical confrontation of different power/knowledge constellations—in order to show that things do not have to be the way they currently are. There is critical work to be done in relation to this, but this is not a process of demystification, of speaking truth to power, but one of eventalization, that is, of the *pluralization* of truth. This also means, and this is quite important for my discussion, that the role of learning in emancipation becomes a radically different one. In one sense we could say that if we follow Foucault there is no longer anything to learn, at least not if we see learning as the condition *for* emancipation. There is, to be more precise, nothing to learn about our objective condition because if we follow Foucault we have to give up the idea that we can make a distinction between our objective condition and our distorted understandings of this condition. Similarly there is nothing to learn about our true human existence because, if we follow Foucault, we have to give up the idea that there is one single true human existence—there are many, which is not to suggest that they are all of equal value or worth, or that human existence is without limits.

While there is, therefore, no longer the suggestion that a particular kind of learning, a learning that discloses the truth, will result in emancipation, this doesn't mean that there is nothing to pick up *from* transgression and pluralization, as long as we bear in mind that these processes themselves are not driven by learning. It is the transgression and pluralization that come first, and what we pick up from our engagement in such emancipatory experiments comes second (and what we do with that is still another matter). In this regard Foucault's approach does suggest a different connection between learning and emancipation. One could also say that given the fact that work of freedom for Foucault is undefined, the process will never come to an end, and in this regard emancipation is a lifelong challenge (not unlike what Freire had in mind, albeit on different terms), that freedom is not a point or a state we can ever reach.

CONCLUSIONS

In this chapter I have tried to raise some critical questions about the notion of "learning," the language of "learning," and the discourse of "learning."

My intention has been to unsettle the positive if not warm feelings educators, educationalists, and people working for change for the better may have for learning, showing the political "work" that is being done through this notion—particularly the political work that keeps us in our place and domesticates and stultifies us, rather than helping us to act differently and be different. I have done this, first of all, by showing some of the problems with the language of learning in educational settings, highlighting the fact that the language of learning tends to obscure those dimensions that make education educational, so to speak. Here I have particularly highlighted the way in which questions about content, purpose, and relation easily disappear from view when we start to talk about education in terms of the individualistic and individualizing process-language of learning. I have, through a discussion of transformations in the field of lifelong learning, tried to highlight how through the very idea of "learning" a substantial amount of political work is done, and that even the very construction of lifelong learning as a "field" is already an example of the politics of learning that is at work. Against this background I have suggested that there is a need for interrupting the politics of learning.

A starting point for such interrupting is to resist the suggestion that learning is a natural process and thus something that simply "occurs"—as if beyond our control. In addition I have highlighted the importance of refusing the very identity of a learner—and more specifically of a lifelong learner—a refusal that at the same time can *expose* and *oppose* the workings of the politics of learning. In the final step I have connected this to the discussion on emancipation in order to show that to give up the notion of learning does not mean to give up on the idea of emancipation. I have used Foucault as an example of what emancipation-without-learning—which for Foucault becomes emancipation-as-transgression—might look like, also showing how my critique of the politics of learning can itself be understood as an attempt at transgression. This is not—or not yet—a wholesale denouncement of the idea of learning, as I still want to be open to the possibility that learning can also work for the good. The crucial issue here is whether it can be up to us to decide whether we learn or not, whether to adopt the learner identity or not, or whether we can only subject ourselves to ongoing demands for learning and ongoing demands to fashion ourselves as lifelong learners—that is, whether we can only succumb to the duty to learn. The crucial question, in other words, is whether we lend anonymous, metaphysical power to the idea of learning, or whether we seize this power in order to make learning as strong or as weak as we want it to be—that is, where learning can work for us, rather than that we have to work for learning, if such an expression makes sense.

CHAPTER FIVE

Emancipation

Equality is not given, nor is it claimed; it is practiced, it is *verified*.
—*Jacques Rancière*

In this chapter I focus in more detail on what I see as one of the more
difficult and certainly one of the more contentious educational questions,
which is the question whether and, if so, how education can contribute to
the freedom of the human subject. This is the question of *emancipation*.
While the idea of emancipation has a respectable history in educational
thought and practice—a history that goes back at least to the Enlightenment—one of the difficulties of connecting education and emancipation has to do with a contradiction that becomes visible when we think
of education as a "powerful intervention" aimed at setting people free.
Thinking about emancipation in this way immediately raises questions
about the power invested in the emancipator as well as about the alleged
unfreedom of those being emancipated. In addition, it raises questions
about the role and status of equality, as the idea of emancipation as a
"powerful intervention" seems to rely on the idea that emancipation is
the process through which a relationship of inequality is transformed into
a relationship of equality—thus making equality into the desired "outcome" of emancipatory education. In this chapter I explore the history of
emancipation in education, identify some of its key contradictions, and,
through a discussion of the work of Jacques Rancière, outline a different
way to engage with the theme of emancipation in education.

77

THE LOGIC OF EMANCIPATION

The idea of emancipation plays a central role in modern educational theories and practices. Many educators see their task not simply as that of modifying or conditioning the behavior of their students. They want their students to become independent and autonomous, to be able to think for themselves, to make their own judgments, and to draw their own conclusions. The emancipatory impetus is particularly prominent in critical traditions and approaches where the aim of education is conceived as that of emancipating students from oppressive practices and structures in the name of social justice and human freedom (see, for example, Gur Ze'ev 2005). What is needed to bring about emancipation, so educators in the critical tradition argue, is an explanation of the workings of power, as it is only when one sees and understands how power operates that it becomes possible to address its influence and, in a sense, escape from it. This is why notions like "demystification" and "liberation from dogmatism" play a central role in critical education (see, for example, Mollenhauer 1976, p. 67; McLaren 1997, p. 218; see also Biesta 1998, 2005). Because it is assumed that power also operates upon people's understandings of the situations they are in, there is an important strand within the critical tradition in which it is argued that emancipation can only be brought about "from the outside," that is, from a position that, itself, is not contaminated by the workings of power. This line of thought goes back to Marxist notions of "ideology" and "false consciousness," and it finds a more recent expression in Pierre Bourdieu's notion of "misrecognition" (see Rancière 2003, pp. 165–202). Hence it becomes the task of the critical educator to make visible what is hidden for those who are the "object" of the emancipatory endeavors of the critical educator. Similarly, the task of critical social science becomes that of making visible what is hidden from the everyday view.

Rancière has raised some important questions about the logic of this particular model of emancipation. Whereas according to this logic the explanation of how the world "really" is leads to emancipation, Rancière has argued that instead of bringing about emancipation, this logic introduces a fundamental *dependency* into the "logic" of emancipation. This is because the ones to be emancipated remain dependent upon the "truth" or "knowledge" revealed to them by the emancipator. The problem, as he puts it in *The Politics of Aesthetics,* is that "where one searches for the hidden beneath the apparent, a position of mastery is established (Rancière 2004, p. 49). In *The Ignorant Schoolmaster* (Rancière 1991a) Rancière has shown in great detail how educational practices based on this logic of emancipation lead to "stultification" rather than emancipation. In other work, particularly *The Philosopher and His*

Poor (Rancière 2003), he has shown that a relationship of dependency is, in a sense, constitutive of Western philosophy and social theory more generally. Rancière's contribution not only lies in highlighting this contradiction within the logic of emancipation. Throughout his career he has worked consistently on the articulation of an alternative approach—an alternative way to understand and "do" emancipation. He has done so using a form that aims to be consistent with his ideas on emancipation in that it is a kind of writing that tries to avoid a position of mastery. Rancière has referred to this as a "topographical" way of writing that articulates "an egalitarian or anarchist theoretical position that does not presuppose this vertical relationship of top to bottom" (Rancière 2004, pp. 49–50; see also Rancière 2009). In this chapter I discuss Rancière's ideas on emancipation from three angles: the angle of political theory, the angle of political practice, and the angle of education. I preface this discussion with a brief overview of the history of emancipation in order to highlight some of the contradictions that Rancière seeks to overcome.

EMANCIPATION AND ITS PREDICAMENTS

The concept of emancipation has its roots in Roman law, where it referred to the freeing of a son or wife from the legal authority of the *pater familias,* the father of the family. *Emancipation* literally means "to give away ownership" (*ex*: away; *mancipium*: ownership). More broadly it means to relinquish one's authority over someone. This implies that the "object" of emancipation, that is, the person to be emancipated, becomes independent and free as a result of the act of emancipation. This is reflected in the legal use of the term today, where emancipation means the freeing of someone from the control of another, particularly in the form of parents relinquishing authority and control over a minor child. In the seventeenth century, emancipation became used in relation to religious toleration, in the eighteenth century in relation to the emancipation of slaves, and in the nineteenth century in relation to the emancipation of women and workers. The Roman use of the term already indicates the link with education, in that emancipation marks the moment when and the process through which the (dependent) child becomes an (independent) adult.

A decisive turn in the trajectory of the idea of emancipation was taken in the eighteenth century when emancipation became intertwined with the Enlightenment and enlightenment became understood as a process of emancipation. We can see this most clearly in Immanuel Kant's essay "What Is Enlightenment?" in which he defined enlightenment as "man's release from his self-incurred tutelage" and saw tutelage or immaturity as "man's inability to make use of his understanding without the direction from another" (Kant 1992 [1784], p. 90). Immaturity is self-incurred, Kant wrote, "when its cause lies not in lack of reason but in lack of resolution and courage to use it without the direction from another" (ibid.). Enlightenment thus entailed a process of becoming independent or autonomous, and for Kant this autonomy was based on the use of one's reason. Kant contributed two further ideas to this line of thinking. First of all he argued that the "propensity and vocation to free think-ing" was not a contingent, historical possibility but should be seen as something that was an inherent part of human nature; it was man's "ultimate destination" and the "aim of his existence" (Kant 1982, p. 701; my translation). To block progress in enlightenment was therefore "a crime against human nature" (Kant 1992 [1784], p. 93). Second, Kant argued that in order for this "capacity" to emerge, we need education. In his view the human being can only become "human"—that is, a rational autonomous being—"through education" (Kant 1982, p. 699; my translation).

Kant's position clearly presents us with a set of interlocking ideas that has become central to modern educational thinking and that has had a pro-found impact on modern educational practice. Kant assumes that there is a fundamental difference between immature and mature beings and that this difference maps onto the distinction between childhood and adulthood. He defines maturity in terms of rationality—the (proper) use of one's reason—and sees rationality as the basis for independence and autonomy. Education is seen as the "lever" for the transition from immaturity to maturity, which, in turn, means that education is intimately connected with the question of freedom. All this is aptly summarized in Kant's formulation of what is known in the literature as the educational paradox, "How do I cultivate freedom through coercion?" (Kant 1982, p. 711; my translation).

From this point onward we can trace the emergence of the notion of emancipation along two related lines: one is educational, the other philosophi-cal. The idea that education is not about the insertion of the individual into the existing order but entails an orientation toward autonomy and freedom played an important role in the establishment of education as an academic discipline in Germany toward the end of the nineteenth and the beginning of the twentieth century (see, for example, Tenorth 2008 [2003]; Biesta 2011a). It also was a central element in "Reformpädagogik," "New Education," and "Progressive Education," which emerged in the first decades of the twentieth century in many countries around the world. In most cases the argument against adaptation was expressed as an argument for the child. Many educa-tionalists followed Rousseau's insight that adaptation to the external societal order would corrupt the child. This led to the idea, however, that a choice for the child could only mean a choice *against* society. This was further supported by theories that conceived of "the child" as a natural category, a "given," and not as something that had to be understood in social, historical, and political terms.

Whereas the idea that education is about the emancipation of the individual child played an important role in the establishment of education as an academic discipline in its own right, the limitations of this view became painfully clear when it turned out that such an approach could easily be adopted by any ideological system, including Nazism and fascism. This is why, after World War II, educationalists—first of all in Germany—began to argue that there could be no individual emancipation without wider societal transformation. This became the central tenet of critical approaches to education. In Germany, a major contribution came from Klaus Mollenhauer, whose critical-emancipatory approach drew inspiration from the (early) work of Jürgen Habermas (see Mollenhauer 1976). Two decades later, but with precursors in the writings of authors like John Dewey, George Counts, and Paulo Freire, a similar body of work emerged in North America, particularly through the contributions of Michael Apple, Henry Giroux, and Peter McLaren. As a critical theory of education, the emancipatory interest of critical pedagogies focuses on the analysis of oppressive structures, practices, and theories. The key idea is that emancipation can be brought about if people gain an adequate insight into the power relations that constitute their situation—which is why, as mentioned, the notion of "demystification" plays a central role in critical pedagogies.

It is here that we can connect the history of the idea of emancipation in education with wider philosophical discussions, at least to the extent to which this history is part of the development of Marxism and neo-Marxist philosophy. It is, after all, a key insight of this tradition that in order to liberate ourselves from the oppressive workings of power and achieve emancipation, we first and foremost need to *expose* how power operates. What the Marxist tradition adds to this—and this, in turn, has influenced critical and emancipatory pedagogies—is the notion of *ideology*. Although the question of the exact meaning of this concept is a topic of ongoing debates (see Eagleton 2007), one of the crucial insights expressed in the concept of ideology is not only that all thought is socially determined—following Karl Marx's dictum that "it is not the consciousness of man that determines their being but, on the contrary, their social being that determines their consciousness" (Marx, quoted in Eagleton 2007, p. 80)—but also, and more importantly, that ideology is thought "which *denies* this determination" (ibid., p. 89). The latter claim is linked to Friedrich Engels's notion of false consciousness: the idea that "the real motives impelling [the agent] remain unknown to him" (Engels, quoted in

Eagleton 2007, p. 89). The predicament of ideology lies in the suggestion that it is precisely because of the way in which power works upon our consciousness that we are unable to see how power works upon our consciousness. This not only implies that in order to free ourselves from the workings of power we need to expose how power works upon our consciousness. It also means that in order for us to achieve emancipation, *someone else,* whose consciousness is not subjected to the workings of power, needs to provide us with an account of our objective condition. According to this logic, therefore, emancipation is ultimately contingent upon the truth about our objective condition, a truth that can only be generated by someone who is positioned outside of the influence of ideology—and in the Marxist tradition this position is considered to be occupied either by science or by philosophy.

What this brief description of emancipation's philosophical and educational emergence begins to reveal are the contours of a certain "logic" of emancipation, a certain way in which emancipation is conceived and understood. There are several aspects to this logic. One is that emancipation requires an intervention from the "outside"—an intervention, moreover, by someone who is not subjected to the power that needs to be overcome. This not only shows that emancipation is understood as something that is *done to* somebody but also reveals that emancipation is based upon a fundamental *inequality* between the emancipator and the one to be emancipated. Equality, in this account, becomes the outcome of emancipation; it becomes something that lies in the future. Moreover, it is this outcome that is used to legitimize the interventions of the emancipator. Whereas this view of emancipation follows more or less directly from philosophical considerations, particularly around the notion of ideology, it is not too difficult to recognize a particular pedagogy in this account as well. This is a pedagogy in which the teacher knows and students do not know *yet,* where it is the task of the teacher to explain the world to the students and where it is the task of the students to ultimately become as knowledgeable as the teacher. We can say, therefore, that the logic of emancipation is also the logic of a particular pedagogy. Although much of this will sound familiar—which, in a sense, proves how influential this modern logic of emancipation has been—this "logic" of emancipation is not without problems; or, to be more precise, it is not without contradictions.

The first contradiction is that although emancipation is orientated toward equality, independence, and freedom, it actually installs *dependency* at the very heart of the "act" of emancipation. The one to be emancipated is, after all, dependent upon the intervention of the emancipator, an intervention based upon a knowledge that is fundamentally inaccessible to the one to be emancipated. When there is no intervention there is, therefore, no emancipation. This does raise the question of when this dependency will actually disappear. Is it as soon as emancipation is achieved? Or should the one who is emancipated remain eternally grateful to his or her emancipator for the "gift" of emancipation? Should slaves remain grateful to their masters for setting them free? Should women remain grateful to men for setting them free? Should children remain grateful to their parents for setting them free? Or could all of them perhaps have asked why they were not considered to be free in the first place?

Modern emancipation is not only based upon dependency—it is also based upon a fundamental *inequality* between the emancipator and the one to be emancipated. According to the modern logic of emancipation, the emancipator is the one who knows better and best and who can perform the act of demystification that is needed to expose the workings of power. According to the modern logic of emancipation, the emancipator does not simply occupy a superior position. It could even be argued that in order for this superiority to exist the emancipator actually needs the inferiority of the one to be emancipated. Again we can ask when this inequality will actually disappear. After all, as long as the master remains a master, the slave can only ever become a former slave or an emancipated slave—but not a master. The slave, in other words, will always lag behind in this logic of emancipation.

The third contradiction within the modern logic of emancipation has to do with the fact that although emancipation takes place in the interest of those to be emancipated, it is based upon a fundamental *distrust* of and *suspicion* about their experiences. The logic of emancipation dictates, after all, that we cannot really trust what we see or feel, but that we need someone else to tell us what it is that we are really experiencing and what our problems really are. We need someone, in other words, who "lifts a veil off the obscurity of things," who "carries obscure depth to the clear surface, and who, conversely, brings the false appearance of the surface back to the secret depths of reason" (Rancière 2010, p. 4). And once more we can ask what it would mean for those "waiting" for their emancipation to be told the "truth" about themselves, their situation, and their problems.

These contradictions not only permeate the general logic of emancipation but also are present in the way in which this logic is manifest in a particular modern or, as Rancière has called it, a particular progressive pedagogy (Rancière 1991a, p. 121; see also Pelletier 2009). I now wish to turn to Rancière's writings in order to show how he has problematized this specific way of understanding emancipation and how he has sought to articulate a different way for understanding and "doing" emancipation and for posing the problem of emancipation in the first place.

EMANCIPATION, POLITICS, AND DEMOCRACY

In *On the Shores of Politics* Rancière characterizes "emancipation" as "escaping from a minority" (Rancière 1995, p. 48). Although this could be read as a formal definition of emancipation as it refers to ending a situation in which one is a minor, the use of the word *escape* already signals a different dynamics from the one outlined above since it associates emancipation with an activity of the one who "achieves" emancipation rather than that it is understood as something that is done *to* somebody. Rancière indeed writes that "nobody escapes from the social minority save by their own efforts" (ibid.). Emancipation is, however, not simply about the move from a minority position to a majority position. It is not a shift in membership from a minority group to a majority group. Emancipation rather entails a "rupture in the order of things" (Rancière 2003, p. 219)—a rupture, moreover, that makes the appearance of subjectivity possible, or, to be more precise, a rupture that *is* the appearance of subjectivity. In this way emancipation can be understood as a process of *subjectification.*[1] Rancière defines subjectification as "the production through a series of actions of a body and a capacity for enunciation not previously identifiable within a given field of experience, whose identification is thus part of the reconfiguration of the field of experience" (Rancière 1999, p. 35).

There are two things that are important in this definition, and they hang closely together. The first thing to emphasize is the supplementary nature of subjectification (Rancière 2003, pp. 224–225). Subjectification, Rancière argues, is different from identification (see Rancière 1995, p. 37). Identification is about taking up an existing identity, that is, a way of being and speaking and of being identifiable and visible that is already possible within the existing order—or, to use Rancière's phrases, within the existing "perceptual field" or "sensible world" (Rancière 2003, p. 226). Subjectification, in comparison, is always "disidentification, removal from the naturalness of a place" (Rancière 1995, p. 36). Subjectification "inscribes a subject name as being different from any identified part of the community" (ibid., p. 37). When Rancière uses the notion of "appearance" in this context it is not, as he puts it, to refer to "the

---

1. While there are definitely similarities between Rancière's use of the notion of subjectification and the way in which I have developed it in my work, and while it is true that Rancière and I are interested in the question of subjectification for the same reasons, the way in which he *theorizes* subjectification is different from how I have approached this issue, particularly in Chapter 1, although the way in which he defines subjectification—that is, as the opposite of being part of an order, which is, in my terms, the opposite of socialization—is identical to my own definition.

illusion masking the reality of reality" (Rancière 2003, p. 224). Subjectification is about the appearance—the "coming into presence," as I have called it elsewhere (Biesta 2006a)—of a way of being that had no place and no part in the existing order of things. Subjectification is therefore a *supplement* to the existing order because it adds something to this order; and precisely for this reason the supplement also *divides* the existing order, the existing "division of the sensible" (Rancière 2003, pp. 224–225).[2] Subjectification thus "redefines the field of experience that gave to each their identity with their lot" (Rancière 1995, p. 40). It "decomposes and recomposes the relationships between the ways of *doing*, of *being* and of *saying* that define the perceptible organization of the community" (ibid.).

Subjectification—and this is the second point—is therefore highly political as it intervenes in and reconfigures the existing order of things, the existing division or distribution of the sensible, that is, of what is "capable of being apprehended by the senses" (Rancière 2004, p. 85). In order to grasp the supplementary nature of subjectification and hence the supplementary nature of politics itself, Rancière makes a distinction within the notion of the political between two concepts: *police* (or police order) and *politics*.[3] Rancière defines police as "an order of bodies that defines the allocation of ways of doing, ways of being, and ways of saying, and that sees that those bodies are assigned by name to a particular place and task" (Rancière 1999, p. 29). It is an order "of the visible and the sayable that sees that a particular activity is visible and another is not, that this speech is understood as discourse and another as noise" (ibid.). Police should not be understood as the way in which the state structures the life of society. It is not, in Habermasian terms, the "grip" of the system on the lifeworld (Habermas 1987), but includes *both*. As Rancière explains, "the distribution of places and roles that defines a police regime stems

---

2. The French word here is *partage*, which can either be translated as "division" or as "distribution." Whereas "distribution" highlights the fact that each particular distribution of the sensible gives everything a place, "division" highlights the fact that subjectification redistributes the distribution of the sensible, and thus both distributes and interrupts.

3. In French Rancière sometimes (but not always and not always consistently) makes a distinction that is difficult to translate (and that has not always been picked up by translators consistently) between *la politique* and *le politique*. The first refers to the domain of politics in the general sense, whereas the latter indicates the moment of the interruption of the police order (*la police* or *l'ordre policier*). The latter, according to Rancière, is the "proper" idea of politics, and in several of his publications he has shown how particularly political philosophy but also particular forms of politics have tried to suppress the political "moment."

as much from the assumed spontaneity of social relations as from the rigidity of state functions" (Rancière 1999, p. 29). "Policing" is therefore not so much about "the 'disciplining; of bodies'" as it is "a rule governing their appearing, a configuration of *occupations* and the properties of the spaces where these occupations are distributed" (ibid.; emphasis in original). One way to read this definition of police is to think of it as an order that is *all-inclusive* in that everyone has a particular place, role, or position in it—that there is an identity for everyone. This is not to say that everyone is included in the running of the order. The point simply is that no one is excluded from the order. After all, women, children, slaves, and immigrants had a clear place in the democracy of Athens, namely, as those who were not allowed to participate in political decision making. In precisely this respect every police order is all-inclusive.

"Politics" then refers to "the mode of acting that perturbs this arrangement" (Rancière 2003, p. 226) and that does so in the name of, or with reference to, equality. Rancière thus reserves the term *politics* "for an extremely determined activity antagonistic to policing: whatever breaks with the tangible configuration whereby parties and parts or lack of them are defined by a presupposition that, by definition, has no place in that configuration" (Rancière 1999, pp. 29–30). This break is manifest in a series of actions "that reconfigure the space where parties, parts, or lack of parts have been defined" (ibid., p. 30). Political activity so conceived is "whatever shifts a body from the place assigned to it.... It makes visible what had no business being seen, and makes heard a discourse where once there was only place for noise" (ibid., p. 30).

> Political activity is always a mode of expression that undoes the perceptible divisions of the police order by implementing a basically heterogeneous assumption, that of a part of those who have no part, an assumption that, at the end of the day, itself demonstrates the sheer contingency of the order [and] the equality of any speaking being with any other speaking being. (Ibid.)

Politics thus refers to the event when two "heterogeneous processes" meet: the police process and the process of *equality* (see ibid.). The latter has to do with "an open set of practices driven by the assumption of equality between any and every speaking being and by the concern to test this equality" (ibid.).[4]

For Rancière politics understood in this way is always *democratic* politics. Democracy is, however, "not a regime or a social way of life"—it is not

---

4. Although some of Rancière's writings may give the impression that he is primarily—or perhaps even exclusively—concerned about questions of inequality

and cannot be, in other words, part of the police order—but should rather be understood "as the institution of politics itself" (ibid., p. 101). Every politics is democratic *not* in the sense of a set of institutions but in the sense of forms of expression "that confront the logic of equality with the logic of the police order" (ibid.). Democracy, so we might say, is a "claim" for equality. Democracy—or, to be more precise, the appearance of democracy—is therefore not simply the situation in which a group who has previously been excluded from the realm of politics steps forward to claim its place under the sun. It is at the very same time the *creation* of a group as a group with a particular identity that didn't exist before. Democratic activity is, for example, to be found in the activity of nineteenth-century workers "who established a collective basis for work relations" that were previously seen as "the product of an infinite number of relationships between private individuals" (ibid., p. 30). Democracy thus establishes new political identities, identities that were not part of and did not exist in the existing order—and in precisely this sense it is a process of subjectification. Or as Rancière puts it, "Democracy is the designation of subjects that do not coincide with the parties of the state or of society" (ibid., pp. 99–100).

This further means that "the place where the people appear" is the place "where a dispute is conducted" (ibid., p. 100). Rancière emphasizes that this dispute—which is the proper "form" of democracy—"is not the opposition of interests or opinions between social parties" (Rancière 2003, p. 225). Democracy, he explains,

> is neither the consultation of the various parties of society concerning their respective interests, nor the common law that imposes itself equally on everyone. The demos that gives it its name is neither the ideal people of sovereignty, nor the sum of the parties of society, nor even the poor and suffering sector of this society. (Ibid.)

The political dispute rather is a conflict "over the very count of those parties" (Rancière 1999, p. 100). It is a dispute between "the police logic of the distribution of places and the political logic of the egalitarian act" (ibid.). Politics

---

in relation to social class, Rancière's configuration of emancipation is definitely not restricted to this. Emancipation is about the verification of the equality of any speaking being with any other speaking being. Dissensus is therefore always about the redistribution of the demarcations between "noise" and "voice," not in terms of a politics of recognition where those with a voice grant a voice to those who until now were considered only to be able to produce "noise," but on the basis of the "simple" claim that one is producing "voice" rather than "noise."

is therefore "primarily a conflict over the existence of a common stage and over the existence and status of those present on it" (ibid., pp. 26–27). The essence of democracy/politics therefore is dissensus rather than consensus (see Rancière 2003, p. 226). But dissensus is not the "opposition of interests or opinions. It is the production, within a determined, sensible world, of a given that is heterogeneous to it" (ibid.). In precisely this sense we could say, therefore, that politics is productive or poetic in that it generates subjectivity rather than that it depends on a particular kind of political subjectivity. This, however, is not about creating "subjects ex nihilo"—politics, as a "mode of subjectification," creates subjects "by transforming identities defined in the natural order" (Rancière 1999, p. 36). It is in this sense that Rancière argues that politics is aesthetics "in that it makes visible what had been excluded from a perceptual field, and in that it makes audible what used to be inaudible" (ibid.).

This is also why Rancière emphasizes that a political subject "is not a group that 'becomes aware' of itself, finds its voice, imposes its weight on society," because establishing oneself as a subject does not happen before the "act" of politics but rather in and through it (ibid., p. 40). Rancière characterizes a political subject as "an operator that connects and disconnects different areas, regions, identities, functions, and capacities existing in the configuration of a given experience—that is, in the nexus of distributions of the police order and whatever equality is already inscribed there, however fragile and fleeting such inscriptions may be" (ibid.). Rancière gives the example of Jeanne Deroin, who in 1849 presents herself as a candidate for a legislative election in which she cannot run. Through this "she demonstrates the contradiction within a universal suffrage that excludes her sex from any such universality" (ibid., p. 41). It is the staging "of the very contradiction between police logic and political logic" (ibid.) that makes this into a political act. It is the "bringing into relationship of two unconnected things [that] becomes the measure of what is incommensurable between two orders," and this produces both "new inscriptions of equality within liberty and a fresh sphere of visibility for further demonstrations" (ibid., p. 42). This is why for Rancière politics is not made up of power relationships but of "relationships between worlds" (ibid.).

It is important to see that for Rancière the point of politics is not to create constant chaos and disruption. Although Rancière would maintain that politics is basically a good thing, this does not mean that the police order is necessarily bad. Although this may not be very prominent in Rancière's work—which means that it is easily overlooked—he does argue that democratic disputes can have a positive effect on the police order in that they produce "inscriptions of equality" (ibid.)—they leave traces behind in the (transformed) police order. This is why Rancière emphasizes that "there is a worse and a better police" (ibid., pp. 30–31). The better one is, however, not the one "that adheres to the supposedly natural order of society or the science of legislators"—it is the one "that all the breaking and entering perpetrated by egalitarian logic has most jolted out of its 'natural' logic" (ibid., p. 31). Rancière thus acknowledges that the police "can produce all sorts of good, and one kind of police may be infinitely preferable to another" (ibid.). But whether police is "sweet and kind" does not make it any less the opposite of politics. This also means that for Rancière politics is quite rare—or as he puts it in *On the Shores of Politics,* politics, and hence democracy, can only ever be "sporadic" (Rancière 1995, p. 41). As politics consists in the interruption of the police order, it can never become that order itself. Politics "is always local and occasional," which is why its "actual eclipse is perfectly real and no political science exists that could map its future any more than a political ethics that would make its existence the object solely of will" (Rancière 1999, p. 139).

It is not difficult to see that the idea of equality permeates everything that Rancière has to say about politics, democracy, and emancipation. What is most significant about Rancière's position is that he does not conceive of equality as something that has to be achieved through politics. For Rancière democracy doesn't denote a situation in which we all have become equals, nor is emancipation the process where we move from inequality to equality, that is, a process through which we overcome inequality and become equals. For Rancière equality is not a goal that needs to be achieved through political or other means. Equality, as he puts it, "is a presupposition, an initial axiom— or it is nothing" (Rancière 2003, p. 223). What we can do—and what, in a sense, drives politics or makes something political—is to test or verify the assumption of equality in concrete situations. Rancière explains that what makes an action political "is not its object or the place where it is carried out, but solely its form, the form in which confirmation of equality is inscribed in the setting up of a dispute, of a community existing solely through being divided" (Rancière 1999, p. 32). For a thing to be political, therefore, "it must give rise to a meeting of police logic and egalitarian logic that is never set up in advance" (ibid.). This means that nothing is political in itself. But anything may become political "if it gives rise to a meeting of these two log- ics" (ibid.). Equality is therefore not a principle that politics needs to press into service. "It is a mere assumption that needs to be discerned within the practices implementing it" (ibid., p. 33). Yet equality only generates politics "when it is implemented in the specific form of a particular case of dissensus" (Rancière 2004, p. 52), and it is then that "a specific subject is constituted, a supernumerary subject in relation to the calculated number of groups, places, and functions of society" (ibid., p. 51).

THE PRACTICE OF EMANCIPATION

If "traditional" emancipation starts from the assumption of inequality and sees emancipation as the act through which someone is made equal through a "powerful intervention" from the outside, Rancière conceives of emancipation as something that people do for themselves. For this they do not have to wait until someone explains their objective condition to them. Emancipation "simply" means to act on the basis of the presupposition—or "axiom"—of equality. In this sense it is a kind of "testing of equality" (Rancière 1995, p. 45). More than a reversal of the traditional way to understand emancipation—which would still accept the legitimacy of the way in which the problem that emancipation needs to resolve is formulated, that is, that it starts from inequality that needs to be overcome—Rancière displaces the "vocabulary" of emancipation and suggests new questions as much as new answers.

The thesis he put forward in his book *The Nights of Labor* (Rancière 1991b) was that working-class emancipation was neither about the importation of scientific thought—that is, knowledge about their objective condition—into the worker's world, nor about the affirmation of a worker culture. It rather was "a rupture in the traditional division [*partage*] assigning the privilege of thought to some and the tasks of production to others" (Rancière 2003, p. 219). Rancière thus showed that the French workers "who, in the nineteenth century, created newspapers or associations, wrote poems, or joined utopian groups were claiming the status of fully speaking and thinking beings" (ibid.). Their emancipation was thus based on "the transgressive will ... to act as if intellectual equality were indeed real and effectual" (ibid.). Rancière argues that what the workers did was different from how emancipation is traditionally conceived. He explains this in terms of the "syllogism of emancipation" (Rancière 1995, p. 45). The major premise of the syllogism is that "all French people are equal before the law" (ibid.). The minor premise is derived from direct experience—for example, the fact that tailors in Paris went on strike because they were not treated as equals with regard to their pay. There is, therefore, a real contradiction. But, as Rancière argues, there are two ways in which this contradiction can be conceived. The first is the way "to which we are accustomed," which says "that the legal/political words are illusory, that the equality asserted is merely a façade designed to mask the reality of inequality" (ibid., p. 46). "Thus reasons the good sense of demystification" (ibid., p. 47). The workers, however, took the other option by taking the major premise seriously. The tailors' strike of 1833 thus took the form of a logical proof. And what had to be demonstrated through their strike was precisely equality.

Writing about this event, Rancière observes that one of the demands of the tailors "seemed strange" as it was a request for "'relations of equality' with the masters" (ibid., pp. 47–48). What they did through this was not denying or trying to overcome the relation of economic dependence that existed between them and their masters. Yet, by making a claim to a different kind of relationship, one of legal equality—by confronting the world of economic inequality with the world of legal equality—they engendered, as Rancière puts it, "a different social reality, one founded on equality" (ibid., p. 48). What is important here—and this is the reason I focus on the detail of the example—is that emancipation in this case was not about overcoming the economic inequality but consisted in establishing a new social relationship, in this case one in which negotiation between workers and their masters became a customary element of their relationship. Rancière summarizes what was at stake here as follows:

> This social equality is neither a simple legal/political equality nor an economic leveling. It is an equality enshrined as a potentiality in legal/political texts, then translated, displaced and maximized in everyday life. Nor is it the whole of equality: it is a way of living out the relation between equality and inequality, of living it and at the same time displacing it in a positive way. (Ibid.)

Emancipation here is therefore not a matter of "making labour the founding principle of the new society." It rather is about the workers emerging from their minority status "and proving that they truly belong to the society, that they truly communicate with all in a common space" (ibid.). They prove through their actions, in other words, "that they are not merely creatures of need, of complaint and protests, but creatures of discourse and reason, that they are capable of opposing reason with reason and of giving their action a demonstrative form" (ibid.). "Self-emancipation," as Rancière calls it in this context, is therefore "self-affirmation as a joint-sharer in a common world" (ibid., p. 49). Rancière adds that "proving one is correct has never compelled others to recognize they are wrong" (ibid.). This is why the "space of shared meaning" is not a space of consensus but of dissensus and transgression. It is a "forced entry" into a common world. This not only means that the call for equality "never makes itself heard without defining its own space" (ibid., p. 50), but also that this call for equality must be articulated "as though the other can always understand [one's] arguments" (ibid.). Rancière warns that those who on general grounds say that the other cannot understand them, that there is no common language, "lose any basis for rights of their own to be recognized" (ibid.). This is why the "narrow path of emancipation" passes between the "acceptance of separate worlds" and the "illusion of consensus"—but it is neither of these options.

Rancière concludes that at the heart of this "new idea of emancipation" thus lies a notion of "equality of intelligences as the common prerequisite of both intelligibility and community, as a presupposition which everyone must strive to validate on their own account" (ibid., p. 51). The "democratic man"—the political subject or subject of politics—is therefore "a being who speaks," and in this regard it is a "poetic being" (ibid., p. 51). This democratic human being, Rancière adds, is capable of embracing "a distance between words and things which is not deception, not trickery, but humanity" (ibid.). The democratic human being is capable of embracing what Rancière refers to as "the unreality of representation," by which he means the unreality of the idea of equality as well as the arbitrary nature of language. But to say that equality is not real doesn't mean that it is an illusion—and precisely here Rancière articulates a position that no longer relies on the need for demystification. He argues that we must start from equality—"asserting equality, assuming equality as a given, working out from equality, trying to work out how productive it can be"—in order to maximize "all possible liberty and equality" (ibid., pp. 51–52). The one who doesn't start from here but instead starts out from distrust, and "who assumes inequality and proposes to reduce it," can only succeed in setting up "a hierarchy of inequalities ... and will produce inequality ad infinitum" (ibid., p. 52).

EDUCATION AND EMANCIPATION

The question whether we should start from the assumption of equality or inequality is not only a question for politics—it is also a central question for education, particularly given the prominent role of education, and a kind of pedagogical thinking more generally, in the Enlightenment "project" of emancipation. One might even argue that the "pedagogy" of traditional emancipation is identical to the pedagogy of traditional education, in that education is often conceived as a practice in which those who do not yet know receive knowledge from those who do know (and are thus dependent upon those who know for their trajectory toward equality and emancipation). Education so conceived thus starts from a fundamental inequality between the one who educates and the one who receives—and needs—education. The question for Rancière is whether this is the only way in which we can understand the logic of education—and hence the logic of emancipation. In his book *The Ignorant Schoolmaster* (Rancière 1991a), he recounts the story of Joseph Jacotot, an exiled French schoolteacher who in the first decades of the nineteenth century developed an educational approach called "universal teaching," which did not conceive of education as a process that starts from inequality in order to bring about equality but that was based on the assumption of the fundamental equality of intelligence of all human beings.

Jacotot's method was the result of a discovery he made when he was asked to teach students whose language he didn't speak. The success of his endeavors taught him that what he had always thought of as being essential for education—explication—was actually not necessary in order for his students to learn. Jacotot thus began to see that explication, rather than being the core of educational activity, actually renders students stupid since, as Rancière explains, to explain something to someone "is first of all to show him he cannot understand it by himself" (Rancière 1991a, p. 6). This is why Rancière refers to explanation as the "myth of pedagogy, the parable of a world divided into knowing minds and ignorant ones" (ibid.). The explicator's "special trick" consists of a "double inaugural gesture" where "he decrees the absolute beginning: it is only now that the act of learning will begin," and, "having thrown a veil of ignorance over everything that is to be learned, he appoints himself to the task of lifting it" (ibid., pp. 6–7). The pedagogical myth thus divides the world into two and divides intelligence into two, "an inferior intelligence and a superior one." Explication, from this point of view, then becomes "enforced stultification" (ibid., p. 7).

Whereas Jacotot didn't teach his students anything—they learned through their own engagement with materials such as books—this didn't mean that they learned without a master; they only learned without a "master explicator" (ibid., p. 12). While "Jacotot had taught them something, he had communicated nothing to them" (ibid., p. 13). What Jacotot had done was summon his students to use their intelligence in a "relationship of will to will" (ibid.). Whereas explication takes place "whenever one intelligence is subordinated to another," emancipation takes place when an intelligence obeys only itself, "even while the will obeys another will" (ibid.). From this perspective the main educational "problem" becomes that of revealing "an intelligence to itself" (ibid., p. 28). What this requires is not explication but attention, that is, making the effort to use one's intelligence. As Rancière writes, what is needed is an "absolute attention for seeing and seeing again, saying and repeating" (ibid., p. 23). The route that students will take in response to this is unknown, but what the student cannot escape, Rancière argues, is "the exercise of his liberty." This is summoned by a three-part question, "What do you see? What do you think about it? What do you make of it? And so on, to infinity" (ibid.).

There are therefore in Jacotot's method only two "fundamental acts" for the master, "He *interrogates,* he demands speech, that is to say, the manifestation of an intelligence that wasn't aware of itself or that had given up," and "he *verifies* that the work of the intelligence is done with attention" (ibid., p. 29; emphasis in original). Rancière emphasizes that the interrogation should not be understood in the Socratic way, where the sole purpose of interrogation is to lead the student to a point that is already known by the master. What is important here is that while this "may be the path to learning," it is "in no way a path to emancipation" (ibid.). Central to emancipation in education, therefore, is the consciousness "of what an intelligence can do when it considers itself equal to any other and considers any other equal to itself" (ibid., p. 39). And this is what constantly needs to be verified, namely, "the principle of the equality of all speaking beings" (ibid.). What needs to be verified is the belief that "there is no hierarchy of *intellectual capacity*" but only "inequality in the *manifestations* of intelligence" (ibid., p. 27; emphasis in original).

Rancière thus concludes that emancipation understood in this way is not something "*given* by scholars, by their explications *at the level of* the people's intelligence"—emancipation is always "emancipation seized, even against the scholars, when one teaches oneself" (ibid., p. 99; emphasis in original). The only thing that is needed here is to summon other people to use their intelligence, which means to verify "the principle of the equality of all speaking beings" (ibid., p. 39). After all, "what stultifies the common people is not the lack of instruction, but the belief in the inferiority of their intelligence" (ibid.). The only thing that is needed is to remind people that they can see and think for themselves and are not dependent upon others who see and think for them.

Would this imply that emancipation depends on the truth of the proposition that all intelligence is equal? This is not how Rancière sees it. For him the task is to see "what can be done under that supposition" (ibid., p. 46). One thing that cannot be done under this supposition is to make emancipation into a social method. Rancière insists that "only a man can emancipate a man" (ibid., p. 102). There are "a hundred ways to instruct, and learning also takes place at the stultifiers' school" (ibid.)—but emancipation is not about learning. Emancipation is about using one's intelligence under the assumption of the equality of intelligence. There is, therefore, "only one way to emancipate," and to this Rancière adds that "no party or government, no army, school, or institution, will ever emancipate a single person" (ibid.) because every institution is always a "dramatization" or "embodiment" of inequality (ibid., p. 105).

The teaching that makes emancipation possible because it starts from the assumption of equality can therefore "only be directed to individuals, never to societies" (ibid.)—and in the final chapter of *The Ignorant Schoolmaster* Rancière recounts how all attempts to turn universal teaching into a method and to institutionalize it failed from the point of view of emancipation.

Rancière is particularly suspicious of attempts to use education—or to be more precise, schools and schooling—to bring about equality. This is of course the ambition of the "progressives" who want to "liberate minds and promote the abilities of the masses" (ibid., p. 121). But the idea of progress so conceived is based on what Rancière refers to as "the pedagogical fiction," which is "the representation of inequality as a *retard* in one's development" (ibid., p. 119; emphasis in original). This puts the educator in the position of always being ahead of the one who needs to be educated in order to be liberated. Rancière warns, however, that as soon as we embark upon such a trajectory—a trajectory that starts from the assumption of inequality—we will never be able to reach equality. "Never will the student catch up with the master, nor the people with its enlightened elite; but the hope of getting there makes them advance along the good road, the one of perfected explications" (ibid., p. 120). The "progressives" wish to bring about equality through "a well-ordered system of public instruction" (ibid., p. 121). Rancière shows how Jacotot's method could even be incorporated in such a system—and actually was adopted in this way, albeit "except in one or two small matters," namely, that the teachers using Jacotot's method were no longer teaching what they didn't know and were no longer starting from the assumption of the equality of intelligence (see ibid., p. 123). But these "small matters" are of course crucial. The choice, therefore, is between "making an unequal society out of equal men and making an equal society out of unequal men" (ibid., 133), and for Rancière the choice is clear. "One only need to learn how to be equal men in an unequal society," as this is what "*being emancipated*" means (ibid.; emphasis in original). But this "very simple thing" is actually "the hardest to understand" because "the new explication—progress—has inextricably confused equality with its opposite" (ibid.). Rancière thus concludes,

> The task to which the republican hearts and minds are devoted is to make an equal society out of unequal men, to *reduce* inequality indefinitely. But whoever takes this position has only one way of carrying it through to the end, and that is the integral pedagogicization of society—the general infantilization of the individuals that make it up. Later on this will be called continuing education, that is to say, the coextension of the explicatory institutions with society. (Ibid.; emphasis in original)

EMANCIPATION AND THE INSTITUTION OF THE SCHOOL

In the preceding sections I have reconstructed Rancière's ideas on emancipation from three different angles: the angle of political theory, the angle of political practice, and the angle of education. Whereas the three accounts differ in emphasis, context, and, to a certain extent, vocabulary, it is not too difficult to see the common set of ideas that runs through them, nor is it hard to discern the underlying "commitment" that informs Rancière's writing. This is not to suggest that it is easy to give a name to this commitment. What emerges from Rancière's work is a commitment to a cluster of interlocking concepts: equality, democracy, emancipation. But the significance of Rancière's work does not lie in a commitment to this set of concepts per se, not in the least because Rancière's "discussion partners"—if this is an appropriate expression[5]—are committed to the very same set of concepts. The ingenuity of Rancière's work lies first and foremost in the fact that he is able to show that what is done under and in the name of equality, democracy, and emancipation often results in its opposite in that it reproduces inequality and keeps people in their place. What matters, therefore, is not *that* we are committed to equality, democracy, and emancipation but *how* we are committed to it and *how* we express and articulate this commitment. Rancière thus introduces a critical difference within the discourse on emancipation, equality, and democracy.

One of Rancière's central insights is that as long as we project equality into the future and see it as something that has to be brought about through particular interventions and activities that aim to overcome existing inequality—such as the education of the masses or the integral pedagogicization of society—we will never reach equality but will simply reproduce inequality. The way out of this predicament is to bring equality into the here and now and act on the basis of the assumption of the equality of all human beings or, as Rancière specifies in *The Ignorant Schoolmaster*, the equality of intelligence of all human beings. To act on the basis of this assumption requires a constant verification of it—not in order to check whether the assumption *is* true *in abstracto*, but in order to *practice* the truth of the assumption, that is, to *make* it true in always concrete situations. As Rancière puts it in *The Ignorant Schoolmaster*, the problem is not to prove or disprove that all intelligence is

---

5. The idea of "discussion partners" would assume that Rancière's work is just one voice within a space that is already defined. Rather than adding his voice to the discussion on emancipation, we might perhaps read Rancière's work as an intervention, or, in his own words, as a staging of dissensus. In this sense we might see Rancière's work itself as a political act or act of politics.

equal but to see "what can be done under that supposition." The name of the practice of the verification of the supposition of equality is "politics." Politics is therefore not the practice that brings about or produces equality, nor is equality the principle that needs to be advanced through the activity of politics. What makes an act political is when it "stages" the contradiction between the logic of the police order and the logic of equality, that is, when it brings into a relationship two unconnected, heterogeneous, and incommensurable worlds: the police order and equality. This is why dissensus lies at the heart of political acts. Dissensus, however, should not be understood as a conflict or "a quarrel" (Rancière 2010, p. 15)—as that would assume that the parties involved in the conflict would already exist and have an identity. Dissensus is "a gap in the very configuration of sensible concepts, a dissociation introduced into the correspondence between ways of being and ways of doing, seeing and speaking" (ibid.).

> Equality is at once the final principle of all social and governmental order and the omitted cause of its "normal" functioning. It resides neither in a system of constitutional forms not in the form of societal mores, nor in the uniform teaching of the republic's children, nor in the availability of affordable products in supermarket displays. Equality is fundamental and absent, timely and untimely, always up to the initiative of individuals and groups who ... take the risk of verifying their equality, of inventing individual and collective forms for its verification. (Ibid.)

This is also why the political act is an act of "supplementary subjects inscribed as surplus in relation to any count of the parts of a society" (Rancière, Panagia, and Bowlby 2001). The political subject—which for Rancière is always also the democratic subject, the *demos*—is therefore constituted in and through the political act, which is why Rancière argues that politics is a process of subjectification. We might say, therefore, that Rancière's central concepts—equality, democracy, and politics—all map onto each other in that the political act consists of the verification of equality and when we do this through the staging of dissensus, democracy "takes place" not as a political regime but as an interruption of the police order. This is also true for the notion of "emancipation" because to *be* emancipated means to act on the basis of the assumption of equality. This has the character of a "forced entry" into a common world that, as I have shown, not only means that the call for equality can only make itself heard by defining its own space but must also proceed on the assumption that the other can always understand one's arguments. Emancipation therefore doesn't appear as the outcome of a particular educational trajectory. Emancipation is about using one's intelligence under the assumption of the equality of intelligence.

CONCLUSIONS

What is important about Rancière's contribution is not only that he presents us with an account of emancipation that is radically different from the traditional account that I have outlined above. The importance of Rancière's contribution lies not only in the fact that he helps us to understand emancipation *differently,* but also in the fact that he is able to overcome the main contradictions within the traditional way to understand and "do" emancipation, particularly the idea that emancipation starts with dependency and that it starts from a fundamental inequality. Rancière's understanding is also no longer based upon a fundamental distrust in the experiences of the ones to be emancipated to the extent that emancipation can only occur if the experiences of the ones to be emancipated are replaced by a "proper" and "correct" understanding. In this regard we can characterize Rancière's account of emancipation as a *weak* account, an account that does not come with a guarantee that emancipators can simply produce the emancipation of those entrusted to them. This is not to suggest that there are no lessons to be learned from history and social analysis. But such lessons are no longer seen as the "motor" for emancipation in that if one draws the "right" conclusions, emancipation will simply follow. Such learning should, in other words, not be staged in terms of the "myth of pedagogy" in which the world is divided into knowing minds (emancipators/explicators) and ignorant ones. The difference here—and this is important in order to appreciate the difference Rancière aims to articulate in our understanding of the practice of emancipatory education—is not that between learning with a master and learning without a master. The difference is between learning with a "master explicator" and learning without a "master explicator." What Rancière is hinting at, in other words, is not a school without teachers, a school without schoolmasters (see also Pelletier 2009); what he sees as the main obstacle to emancipation is the position of the "master explicator."[6] There is, therefore, still authority within emancipatory education, but this authority is not based

---

6. This also means—and this is a point that is often overlooked by readers of Rancière—that Rancière's argument is not an argument against the role of explanation in education per se; after all, one might say that there is a lot of explanation going on in Rancière's own writings. The only point with regard to explanation is that it is not the avenue toward emancipation.

on a difference of knowledge or insight or understanding. "The ignorant schoolmaster exercises no relation of intelligence to intelligence. He or she is only an authority, only a will that sets the ignorant person down a path, that is to say to instigate a capacity already possessed" (Rancière 2010, pp. 2–3).

And all this is not only an issue for the school. It is at the very same time, and perhaps first of all, an issue for society and the way in which we conceive of emancipation at large. Rancière's ideas imply a critique of a particular "logic" of emancipation in which it is assumed that emancipation requires a "powerful intervention" from the outside—an intervention, moreover, based on explanation. In this regard we might say that Rancière's critique is aimed at any situation in which explanation emerges as the key to emancipation—the school is one example of this, but this particular "logic" of schooling can happen in many other places too, even to the extent to which society itself becomes modeled on the explanatory logic of schooling (on this see Bingham and Biesta 2010, chapter 8, "The World Is Not a School"). In this way Rancière's critique is first and foremost a critique of a particular logic of emancipation, a logic exemplified in a particular notion of schooling but not confined to the institution of the school.

CHAPTER SIX

Democracy

Plurality is the condition of human action.

—*Hannah Arendt*

If Rancière helps us to see how education and politics are intimately connected if what is "at stake" is the question of emancipation, Hannah Arendt, who forms my discussion partner in this chapter, is an author who comes from the opposite end, as she has been one of the most outspoken critics of the idea that education and politics may have anything to do with each other. She takes the view that the realm of education should be "divorced" from all other realms, and most of all from the realm of political life. Arendt thus poses a real challenge to anyone who is interested in the interrelationships between education, emancipation, democracy, and politics. Yet this challenge is important because it can help to bring into light some of the assumptions upon which arguments for and against particular constellations of democratic education are based. One such assumption—as I will show in this chapter—has to do with what Rancière refers to as the "pedagogical fiction," which is "the representation of inequality as a *retard* in one's development" (Rancière 1991a, p. 119). This "pedagogical fiction" is a manifestation of a much wider problem in educational discourse and practice, which is the tendency to think of education entirely in psychological terms and, more specifically, in terms of psychological *development*.

In this chapter I show how Arendt's argument for the strict separation of the domain of education from the domain of politics is informed by such a "developmental" understanding of education. While these assumptions play a central role in those parts of Arendt's work where she discusses education explicitly, they disappear when Arendt writes about politics. Here the "tone" of her work is distinctively political and, more important for the wider argument in this book, also distinctively *existential* in that her focus is on the question of what it means—as I put it—to exist politically, that is, *to exist under the condition of plurality.* I will use the latter angle to construct an argument against Arendt's case for the separation of education from the field of democratic politics—which, as I will try to make clear, is at the very same time an argument that takes the whole question of democratic education away from psychological developmentalism and locates it firmly in the domain of human action (understood in the Arendtian sense of the word; see below). By making the question of democracy existential rather than developmental I also suggest a reading that makes the connection between education and democracy a weak one, that is, one where the idea is not that education can develop or, even worse, produce democratic persons but where there is an ongoing interest in promoting those situations—those forms of human togetherness in which, as Arendt puts it, freedom can appear.

DEMOCRATIC EDUCATION AND THE PROBLEM OF DEVELOPMENTALISM

The question of the role of education in democratic societies has been an issue of ongoing concern, both from the side of educators and educationalists and from the side of politicians and policy makers. What is at stake in these discussions are not only technical questions about the proper shape and form of democratic education and education for democratic citizenship, but also more philosophical questions about the nature of democracy and the configurations of citizenship within democratic societies. However, a question that has received far less attention in the literature is that of the *relationship* between education and democracy. The prevailing view has been that this relationship should be seen as an *external* relationship in which education is understood as the trajectory that brings about or creates democratic citizens (see Biesta and Lawy 2006; Biesta 2007a). Even in those cases in which it is argued that the only way toward democratic citizenship is through engagement in democratic processes and practices, the assumption often is that such engagement should generate the democratic person, that is, the person who possesses democratic knowledge, skills, values, and dispositions (see, for example, Apple and Beane 1995). We might refer to this as a *psychological* view of democratic education because the educational task is conceived as that of producing a particular kind of individual by working upon the individual's mind and body. Democratic education thus becomes a form of moral education since its task is seen as that of bringing about an individual with a particular set of moral qualities and dispositions (for such a view, see, for example, Kerr 2005, who refers to this set of qualities as the "citizenship dimensions").

Although this set of assumptions continues to play an important role in educational practices around the world, it is not without problems. From an *educational* point of view one of the main problems with the idea that the relationship between education and democracy should be seen as an external relationship is that it makes it difficult to acknowledge the political nature of the educational processes at stake. By positioning democracy at the endpoint of democratic education, as something that comes *after* education, it is suggested that the learning that matters in these processes is itself not affected by the characteristics (and troubles) of democratic politics. From a *democratic* point of view one of the problems with this line of thinking is that it is based on the assumption that the guarantee for democracy lies in the existence of a properly educated citizenry, so that once all citizens are properly educated, democracy will simply follow.

The question that I wish to explore is whether it is possible to think of the relationship between education and democracy differently. This is not only important in order to be able to acknowledge the political nature of democratic education; it is also important in order to be able to acknowledge the political "foundation" of democratic politics itself. While I see Hannah Arendt as one of the most "political" thinkers of the twentieth century,[1] she is also one of the most outspoken critics of the idea that education and politics should have anything to do with each other—which poses a real problem for anyone who wishes to mine Arendt's work in the field of democratic education (see Gordon 1999, 2002; Pols 2001; Schutz 2002). As she asserted in her essay "The Crisis in Education," "We must decisively divorce the realm of education from the others, most of all from the realm of public, political life" (Arendt 1977a, p. 195). I believe that in making this claim, Arendt fell prey to a mistake that is not uncommon when philosophers turn to education, albeit that philosophers are not the only ones who make this mistake. The mistake is to assume that the only available vocabulary for talking about education is a psychological one, that is, a vocabulary of "development," "preparation," "identity," and "control," so that notions like "action," "plurality," "subjectivity," and "freedom" only begin to matter once children have gone through a

---

1. I refer to Arendt as a political thinker and not a political philosopher because she explicitly rejected the latter label (see Arendt 2003).

particular developmental and educational trajectory and have reached the state of adulthood. The mistake, to put it differently, is to assume that "childhood" and "adulthood" are natural categories and not social and political ones, and that freedom only has to do with the latter and not with the former.

What I aim to show in this chapter is that Arendt herself provides one of the most compelling arguments against the idea that the relationship between education and democratic politics can only be mediated psychologically. Central to this argument is Arendt's contention that the basis for the public realm, the realm "where freedom can appear," is not moral—it is not the outcome of successful moral socialization—but is itself political. This means that for Arendt the appearance of freedom is not contingent upon the existence of individuals who possess a particular set of moral qualities but depends upon a particular way of being together, namely, "being-together-in-plurality." The upshot of this is that freedom cannot be produced educationally but can only be achieved politically. It is precisely this difference, as I will argue, that provides us with a way of understanding democratic education that is nonpsychological and nonmoral but nonetheless thoroughly educational.

ACTION, FREEDOM, AND PLURALITY

Arendt's philosophy centers on an understanding of human beings as *active* beings, that is, as beings whose humanity is not simply defined by their capacity to think and reflect but where being human has everything to do with what one *does*. Arendt distinguishes between three modalities of the active life (the *"vita activa"*): labor, work, and action. *Labor* is the activity that corresponds to the biological processes of the human body. It stems from the necessity to maintain life and is exclusively focused on the maintenance of life. It does so in endless repetition, "one must eat in order to labor and must labor in order to eat" (Arendt 1958, p. 143). Labor, therefore, creates nothing of permanence. Its efforts must be perpetually renewed so as to sustain life. *Work*, on the other hand, has to do with the ways in which human beings actively change their environment and through this create a world that is characterized by its durability. Work has to do with production and creation and hence with "instrumentality." It is concerned with making and therefore "entirely determined by the categories of means and end" (ibid.). In this mode of activity the human being—as *"homo faber"* rather than as *"animal laborans"*—is the builder of stable contexts within which human life can unfold. While labor and work have to do with instrumentality and necessity and with aims and ends that are external to the activity, action, the third mode of the *vita activa,* is an end in itself, and its defining quality is *freedom.*

For Arendt, to act first of all means to take initiative, to begin something new, to bring something new into the world. Arendt characterizes the human being as an *initium*: a "begin*ning* and a begin*ner*" (Arendt 1977b, p. 170). She argues that what makes each of us unique is not the fact that we have a body and need to labor to maintain our body, nor the fact that through work we change the environment we live in. What makes each of us unique is our potential to do something that has not been done before. This is why Arendt writes that every act is in a sense a miracle, "something which could not be expected" (ibid., p. 170). Arendt likens action to the fact of birth, since with each birth something "uniquely new" comes into the world (see Arendt 1958, p. 178). But it is not only at the moment of birth that something new comes into the world. We *continuously* bring new beginnings into the world through what we do and say. "With word and deed," Arendt writes, "we insert ourselves into the human world and this insertion is like a second birth" (ibid., pp. 176–177). It is through action—and *not* through labor and work—that our "distinct uniqueness" is revealed.

Action is therefore intimately connected with freedom. Arendt emphasizes, however, that freedom should not be understood as a phenomenon of the will, that is, as the freedom to do whatever we choose to do, but that we should instead conceive of it as the freedom "to call something into being which did not exist before" (Arendt 1977b, p. 151). The subtle difference between freedom as sovereignty and freedom as beginning has far-reaching consequences. The main implication is that freedom is not an "inner feeling" or a private experience but something that is by necessity a public and hence a political phenomenon. "The *raison d'être* of politics is freedom," Arendt writes, "and its field of experience is action" (ibid., p. 146). Arendt stresses again and again that freedom needs a "public realm" to make its appearance (see ibid., p. 149). Moreover, freedom only exists *in action,* which means that human beings *are* free—as distinguished from their "possessing the gift of freedom"—as long as they act, "neither before nor after" (ibid., p. 153). But how can freedom appear?

In order to answer this question it is crucial to see that "beginning" is only half of what action is about. Although it is true that we reveal our distinct uniqueness through what we do and say, we should not think of this as a process through which we disclose some kind of preexisting identity. Arendt writes that "nobody knows whom he reveals when he discloses himself in deed or word" (Arendt 1958, p. 180). Everything here depends on how others will respond to our initiatives. This is why Arendt writes that the agent is not an author or a producer, but a subject in the twofold sense of the word, namely, one who began an action and the one who suffers from and is subjected to its consequences. The basic idea of Arendt's understanding of action is therefore very simple: *we cannot act in isolation.* If I were to begin something but no one would respond, nothing would follow from my initiative and, as a result, my beginnings would not come into the world. *I* would not appear in the world. But if I begin something and others do take up my beginnings, I *do* come into the world, and in precisely this moment I *am* free.

This means that our "capacity" for action—and hence our freedom—crucially depends on the ways in which others take up our beginnings. The "problem" is, however, that others respond to our initiatives in ways that are unpredictable. As Arendt puts it, we always act upon beings "who are capable of their own actions" (ibid., p. 190). Although this frustrates our beginnings, Arendt emphasizes again and again that the "impossibility to remain unique masters of what [we] do" is at the very same time the condition—and the *only* condition—under which our beginnings can come into the world (ibid., p. 244). We can of course try to control the ways in which others respond to our beginnings—and Arendt acknowledges that it is tempting to do so. But if we were to do so, we would deprive other human beings of their opportunities to begin. We would deprive them of their opportunities to act, and hence we would deprive them of their freedom. Action is therefore never possible in isolation. Arendt even goes so far as to argue that "to be isolated is to be deprived of the capacity to act" (ibid., p. 188). In order to be able to act we therefore need others—others who respond to our initiatives and take up our beginnings. This also means, however, that action is never possible without plurality. As soon as we erase plurality—as soon as we erase the otherness of others by attempting to control how they respond to our initiatives—we deprive others of their actions and their freedom, and as a result we deprive ourselves of our possibility to act, and hence of our freedom. This is why Arendt maintains that "plurality is the condition of human action" (ibid., p. 8).

Arendt thus provides us with a highly political understanding of freedom. This is not only because she sees freedom in terms of our appearance in the public realm and not, as is the case in liberal political theory, as something that is ultimately private. It is also, and more importantly—because she shows that our freedom is fundamentally interconnected with the freedom of others—contingent upon the freedom of others. The latter is not to be understood as just an empirical fact but rather as the normative core of Arendt's philosophy. Arendt is committed to a world in which everyone has the opportunity to act, appear, and be free. An important implication of this is that the public domain, the domain in which freedom can appear, should not be understood in physical terms but denotes a particular quality of human interaction. As Arendt explains,

> The *polis,* properly speaking, is not the city-state in its physical location; it is the organization of the people as it arises out of acting and speaking together, and its true space lies between people living together for this purpose, no matter where they happen to be.... It is the space of appearance in the widest sense of the word, namely, the space where I appear to others as others appear to me, where men exist not merely like other living or inanimate things but make their appearance explicitly. (Ibid., pp. 198–199)

The "space of appearance" comes into being "when men are together in the manner of speech and action" (ibid., p. 199). This means that "unlike the spaces which are the work of our hands," that is, the spaces created through work, "it does not survive the actuality of the movement which brought it into being, but disappears ... with the disappearance or arrest of the activities themselves" (ibid., p. 199).

Action is thus characterized by the fact that it is "entirely dependent upon the constant presence of others" (ibid., p. 23). This is one of the ways in which Arendt makes a distinction between the private and the public realm, in that labor and work do "not need the presence of others" (ibid., p. 22), whereas action does.[2] In this way we could say that Arendt allocates a proper place to each dimension of the *vita activa.* The private, the realm of the *oikos* or household, is concerned with the satisfaction of material need by means of labor and work carried out under the rule of necessity. The public, as Arendt puts it, "signifies the world itself, in so far as it is common to all of us" (ibid., p. 52). It is, however, "not identical with the earth or with nature" but is related "to the human artifact, the fabrication of human hands, as well as to affairs which go on among those who inhabit the man-made world together" (ibid.). The "most elementary meaning" of the two realms, the private and the public, therefore is "that there are things that need to be hidden and others that need to be displayed publicly if they are to exist at all" (ibid., p. 73). To the extent to which work is about the fabrication of a common world, "a

---

2. Arendt's point is actually slightly more subtle in that she argues that *all* human activities "are conditioned by the fact that men live together" (Arendt 1958, p. 22). Labor and work can be conducted without the presence of others, although "a being laboring in complete solitude would not be human but an *animal laborans,*" just as a being "working and fabricating and building a world inhabited only by himself would still be a fabricator, though not *homo faber*" (ibid.).

world of things [that] is between those who have it in common, as a table is located between those who sit around it" (ibid.), it has a public quality. But unlike action, it does not need "the presence of others," which shows precisely why work is not political in the sense in which action is.

Whereas there is a clear hierarchy in the way Arendt depicts the three modes of the *vita activa,* central to her critique of modernity is the assertion that in modernity this hierarchy has been reversed. Arendt is particularly concerned about the "rise of the social," which concerns the "victory of the *animal laborans*" and the assertion of life itself as "the ultimate point of reference" and "the highest good" (ibid., p. 320). The rise of the social thus coincides with the demise of the political. One way to read Arendt's project is as an attempt to reclaim a space for what is distinctly political, which, in her view, is at the same time what is distinctly human. One question this raises is where education sits in this configuration.

THE CRISIS IN EDUCATION

Arendt articulated her views on education most prominently in an essay first published in 1958 called "The Crisis in Education" (Arendt 1977a). In it, as I mentioned above, Arendt argues that the proper location of education is not to be found in the public realm and that in this sense education should *not* be understood politically. Arendt's argument that the realm of education "must be divorced from the others, most of all from the realm of public, political life" (ibid., p. 195), does not mean, however, that its proper place lies in the private sphere. Arendt clearly rejects the suggestion that education is only about life. She writes, "If the child were … simply a not yet finished living creature, education would be just a function of life and would need to consist in nothing save that concern for the sustenance of life and that training and practice in living that all animals assume in respect to their young" (ibid., p. 185). Whereas such sustenance is important for the (younger) child, that is, for children "who are still at the stage where the simple fact of life and growth outweighs the factor of personality" and who "by nature require the security of concealment in order to mature undisturbed," the situation is "entirely different in the sphere of educational tasks directed no longer toward the child but toward the young person, the newcomer and the stranger, who has been born into an already existing world which he does not know" (ibid., p. 188). The situation is entirely different when the focus is not so much on "responsibility for the vital welfare of a growing thing as for what we generally call the free development of characteristic qualities and talents," that is, "the uniqueness that distinguishes every human being from every other" (ibid., p. 189). It is here that Arendt sees a specific task for the school. But whereas the domain of the school is not private, that is, not focused on the maintenance of life, it is not public either. For Arendt the school is a kind of "halfway" institution. It is "the institution that we interpose between the private domain of home and the world in order to make the transition from the family to the world possible at all" (ibid., pp. 188–189).

Part of the task of the school is to gradually introduce the child to the world (see ibid., p. 189). In this process care must be taken "that this new thing comes to fruition in relation to the world as it is" (ibid.). Arendt argues that educational activity therefore has to have an element of conservatism "in the sense of conservation" because it is "of the essence of the educational activity [to] cherish and protect ... the child against the world" (ibid., p. 192), just as it is the task of education to protect the world "from being overrun and destroyed by the onslaught of the new that burst upon it with each new generation" (ibid., p. 186). It is, therefore, exactly for the sake "of what is new and revolutionary in every child [that] education must be conservative: it must preserve this newness and introduce it as a new thing into the world" (ibid., p. 193). For Arendt this also means that educators here "stand in relation to the young as representatives of a world for which they must assume responsibility although they themselves did not make it, and even though they may secretly or openly, wish it were other than it is" (ibid., p. 189). To forfeit this responsibility—a responsibility that, according to Arendt, comes with the fact that children are not simply summoned into life but are born into the world—would turn education into (collective) learning and would in this respect mean the end of education (see also Biesta 2004b). This is not only at the center of Arendt's critique of progressive education (see Arendt 1977a, pp. 180–185). It is also central to Arendt's diagnosis of the "crisis in education," which she sees first and foremost as a refusal of adults to take responsibility for the world.

In education this responsibility for the world "takes the form of authority" (ibid., p. 189), and it is this authority that characterizes the special nature of the relationships in education between adult and children, between "old-timers" and "newcomers." Educational authority, Arendt warns, should not be confused with oppression—"though even this absurdity of treating children as an oppressed minority in need of liberation has actually been tried out in modern educational practice" (ibid., p. 190). The reason for this is that if we emancipate children from the authority of adults and leave them to their own devices, we do not free children but rather subject them "to a much more terrifying and truly tyrannical authority, the tyranny of the majority" (ibid., p. 181). Arendt argues that "there are very few grown people who can endure such a situation," but "children are simply and utterly incapable of it" (ibid., p. 181). Because they are children, they can neither reason against the tyranny of the group nor, in the case of progressive education, can they "flee to any other world because the world of adults is barred from them" (ibid., pp. 181–182). For Arendt, conservation, authority, and responsibility as a responsibility for the world are therefore necessary in education so that children stand a chance of "undertaking something new, something unforeseen by us" (ibid., p. 196). But this *only* holds for the realm of education, that is, "for the relations between grown-ups and children," and not "for the realm of politics, where we act among and with adults as equals" (ibid., p. 192). From the educational angle Arendt warns that if we force children to expose themselves "to the light of a public existence" too early, that is, when they still are "in process of becoming but not yet complete" (ibid., p. 187), we prevent them from ever bringing their beginnings into the world. From a political angle, however, a conservative attitude is problematic because in order to "preserve the world against the mortality of its creators and inhabitants it must be constantly set right anew" (ibid., p. 192).

ARENDT'S DEVELOPMENTALISM

The foregoing paragraphs reveal that Arendt offers us more than a simple pronouncement that education and politics have nothing to do with each other and should have nothing to do with each other. She provides a detailed and challenging set of arguments to support her claim that the educational and the political realms should be kept apart. Relationships in the educational realm are characterized by authority and focus on conservation. This is partly because children as newcomers cannot be held responsible for the existing world. It is the adult/educator who has to carry this responsibility, who has to stand for the world and has to represent the world to newcomers by saying, "This is our world" (ibid., p. 189). Relationships in the political realm, in comparison, are characterized by equality and a focus on renewal. It is here that there is an opportunity for taking "an equal responsibility for the course of the world" (ibid., p. 190), although, as Arendt observes, in the modern world it may also be the case that no one wishes to take any responsibility for the common world (ibid., p. 190).

Arendt's argument is, however, not only about the difference between educational and political *relationships*. It is also based on a particular view of childhood (and hence of adulthood) in which the child is seen as "a developing human being" and childhood is seen as "a temporary stage, a preparation for adulthood" (ibid., p. 184). While Arendt doesn't deny that children and adults live together in the world, she does maintain that there is a fundamental distinction between children and adults so that "one can neither educate adults nor treat children as though they were grown up" (ibid., p. 195). For Arendt—and this is an important point for the argument I wish to make—education thus always operates in the domain of *preparation*. It is only when the state of adulthood is reached—that is, when education has come to its end—that political life can begin. This also explains why the word *freedom* doesn't appear in Arendt's argument, since for her freedom is a political concept that only exists in the realm of politics. For Arendt, freedom simply isn't an educational concept.

Although Arendt's views are consistent and to a certain extent also plausible, they leave one important question unanswered. This is the question of where education ends and politics begins. Arendt's own answer to this question is based on a distinction between childhood and adulthood, although she hastens to add that where the line between the two actually falls "cannot be determined by a general rule; it changes often, in respect to age, from country to country, from one civilization to another, and also from individual to individual" (ibid., p. 195). Notwithstanding this, what her approach does reveal is that she seeks to answer this question within a *temporal* framework, that is, as a question of (psychological) development and transition. If we were to follow this lead, it immediately raises the question, What marks the transition point from childhood to adulthood? When, to put it differently, is the child "ready" for politics? Is it when the child has sufficiently grown? Is it when the child has become capable of reason? Is it when the child is able to take responsibility for the world?

The issue I wish to raise here is not what the right answer to these questions is, and even less what Arendt's answer may have been. The more important issue, in my view, is whether this is the right question. Should we conceive of the difference between education and politics in temporal and developmental terms, that is, in terms of a distinction between childhood and adulthood—or, to be more precise, in terms of a *temporal* distinction between childhood and adulthood, where adulthood is the stage that comes *after* childhood? On this point I wish to make two observations.

There is, of course, some plausibility in Arendt's argument that (young) children may not be able to cope with the "tyranny of the majority" that she sees as a characteristic of those situations where children are left together, without the authority of an adult. But Arendt herself already notes that there are very few grown-up people who can actually endure such situations. This already shows that the issue here is not about the distinction between children and adults but about the difference between modes of human togetherness that are characterized by the "tyranny of the majority" and modes of human togetherness in which freedom can appear. Perhaps Arendt would want to argue that being an adult is a necessary but not sufficient condition for the latter, which would suggest that freedom can never appear when children are together. But putting the case in this way mainly shows that the distinction between "child" and "adult" is in fact a distinction of definition, in that "adults" are those who are capable of creating a political space, whereas "children" are those who are not capable of this. But we all know of many "adults" who are *not* capable of this—and we would of course hesitate to call them children. This suggests that to ask when the child is ready for politics may well be the wrong question. The question we should ask is, What are the conditions for politics, action, and freedom? (And developmental psychology cannot give us an answer to this question, because freedom is not something that can be educationally produced; it can only be politically achieved.)

A similar conclusion follows when we approach the question from the opposite end. By keeping the realm of education apart from the realm of politics, Arendt seems to assume that the dynamics of the realm of politics—the dynamics of beginning and response, of action-in-plurality—either do not happen in the realm of education or can be held at bay by the educator. Only if we were to assume that children are simply not capable of word and deed but only produce "noise" can it be argued that action and freedom will never appear among children. And just as it is unlikely to assume that when children are together, freedom will never appear and action will never occur—unless, again, we would take this as our definition of a child—it is unlikely to assume that when adults are together, freedom will always appear and action will always occur—unless that is how we would want to define adulthood. Again we arrive at the conclusion that the conditions for politics, action, and freedom do not simply *coincide* with the developmental stage called adulthood. Just as being an adult is no guarantee for action and freedom, being a child is no guarantee for the absence of action and freedom. The question, again, is, What are the conditions for politics, action, and freedom?

Whereas I do believe that Arendt is right in her analysis of what underlies the crisis in education—viz., the refusal of adults to take responsibility for the world—I do not believe that her argument for the separation between the sphere of education and the sphere of politics is valid. Or at least, I do not think that the way in which she makes the distinction between the two spheres is convincing. The problem lies in Arendt's "developmentalism," that is, in her reliance upon an unquestioned distinction between "child" and "adult." This seems to make it impossible for her to acknowledge the political dimensions of educational processes and practices. At the same time, it seems to allow her to think of the conditions for politics, action, and freedom in psychological terms, that is, in terms of a readiness for politics that coincides with the transition from childhood to adulthood. In the next section I will show that Arendt herself provides arguments against the idea that the relationship between education and politics can only be mediated psychologically. This, as I will argue, opens up a different way to think about the relationship between education and democratic politics.

POLITICAL EXISTENCE

As I have indicated, one of the constant themes in Arendt's writings is a concern for freedom—or, to put it in Arendtian terms, a concern for the space where freedom can appear, a space where people can act and where action is possible. If this is lost, we slip back into an existence that is no longer about our distinct uniqueness, but only about the maintenance and preservation of life (in the Arendtian sense of the word). We slip back into an existence that in this respect is no longer human. There is, therefore, much at stake in the question of how we can bring about a space in which freedom can appear. Arendt argues that for this we do not simply need a public realm. What we need is a public realm with a particular quality, because freedom can only ever appear under the condition of *plurality*. The key question with regard to political life, therefore, is to determine what "makes it bearable for us to live with other people, strangers, forever, in the same world, and makes it possible for them to bear with us" (Arendt 1994, p. 332). In her essay "Understanding and Politics" (Arendt 1994), Arendt relates this specific question to the task of understanding. Understanding, as she puts it, "as distinguished from correct information and scientific knowledge is . . . an unending activity by which, in constant change and variation, we come to terms with, reconcile ourselves to reality, that is, try to be at home in the world" (ibid., pp. 307–308). Understanding is neither the unmediated expression of direct experience nor mere knowledge. Instead it shares something with judging (see ibid., p. 313). Understanding "is the specifically human way of being alive, for every single person needs to be reconciled to a world into which he was born a stranger and in which, to the extent of his distinct uniqueness, he always remains a stranger" (ibid., p. 308). Arendt thus hints at a way of existing together that is distinctly political because it is committed to existing *together*—it is not our private existence—and to doing so in a way that maintains *plurality*.[3] It is about a way of existing together in which we bear with strangers and they bear with us.

It might seem plausible to assume that what makes such a way of existence possible are qualities such as tolerance and respect, which ultimately are *moral* qualities. This would mean, as Hansen suggests, "that morality is the primary basis and expression of our capacity to bear with each other as strangers" (Hansen 2005, p. 5). But in "Understanding and Politics" Arendt develops a different way of looking at this that focuses on the distinction between the public and social realm, between laws and customs and ultimately between politics and morality (see Hansen 2005, p. 5). Arendt starts her argument by noting that nations begin to decline when lawfulness is undermined. When this happens, what holds a political body together is its customs and traditions, its "patterns of morality" (see ibid.). Arendt argues, however, that "tradition can be trusted to prevent the worst only for a limited period of time. Every incident can destroy customs and morality, which no longer have their foundation in lawfulness, every contingency must threaten a society which is no longer guaranteed by citizens" (Arendt 1994, p. 315). There are therefore real dangers for a political body "held together by customs and tradition, that is the mere binding force of morality" (ibid.). This suggests "a potentially shocking claim" (Hansen 2005, p. 6), namely, that "understanding, judging, bearing with strangers itself not only do not articulate a morality, they stand on a different foundation from it" (ibid.). Instead of thinking that it is morality that makes politics possible, Arendt suggests that it is political existence that makes morality possible. Arendt had good reasons for taking this stance, since she had convincingly shown "that under Nazi rule those who could think and judge for themselves were more likely to resist the regime than those who possessed a moral code" (ibid.).

The question therefore is what it means to "exist politically." The short answer to this question is that to exist politically means to exist together-in-plurality. It means to act "in concert" (Arendt 1958, p. 57) without eradicating plurality. But there are different ways in which existing together-in-plurality can be understood (and, for that matter, can be "done"). The question therefore is how common action is possible given "the simultaneous presence of innumerable perspectives and aspects in which the common world presents itself and for which no common measurement or denominator can ever be devised" (Arendt 1958, p. 57). At this point it is important to see that whereas Arendt would reject the idea that we can only act "in concert" on the basis of a common

---

3. I deliberately use the phrase "*existing* politically" and not "*living* politically" because in Arendt's vocabulary the latter is an oxymoron.

identity, she does acknowledge that common action is not possible if we simply let plurality exist. Common action is not possible on the basis of *mere* plurality. Arendt's understanding of existing politically thus clearly implies a rejection of what I wish to call "disconnected pluralism." For Arendt, connection is possible, but always only as connection-in-difference. Common action under the condition of plurality is therefore not to be conceived as an antagonistic struggle in which "beginners" simply enforce their own beginnings upon others. Common action requires decision and hence deliberation and judgment. But just as Arendt rejects *pluralism-without-judgment,* she also rejects what I suggest to call *judgment-without-plurality.* She rejects, in other words, any form of political judgment that situates itself outside of the web of plurality.

Arendt articulates her ideas on political judgment in a discussion of Kant's *Critique of Judgment* (Arendt 1982). Political judgment, since it is concerned with human togetherness, has to be representative. It requires, in other words, a form of generality or, with the word that Arendt prefers, it requires *publicity,* which she defines as "the testing that arises from contact with other people's thinking" (ibid., p. 42). Contrary, however, to the idea of representative thinking as a form of *abstracting* from one's own contingent situation in order to think in the place "of any other man"—which is the position Kant advocated—Arendt approaches representative thinking as a form of *multiperspective understanding* (see Disch 1994, pp. 152–153). For Arendt "it is not abstraction but considered attention to particularity that accounts for 'enlarged thought'" (ibid., p. 153). Representative thinking is therefore closely connected with particulars, "with the particular conditions of the standpoints one has to go through in order to arrive at one's own 'general standpoint'" (Arendt 1982, p. 44).

In order to achieve this, the act of judgment must consist of more than thinking and decision. It needs the help of the *imagination.* But unlike Kant, who assumed that imagination is only needed to establish a critical distance that makes it possible to assume a universal standpoint, Arendt argues that we need imagination both for "putting things in their proper distance" *and* for "bridging the abysses to others" (Disch 1994, p. 157). The latter activity of the imagination in judging is called *visiting.* As Disch explains, visiting involves "constructing stories of an event from each of the plurality of perspectives that might have an interest in telling it and"—and this "and" is crucial— "imagining how I would respond as a character in a story very different from my own" (ibid., p. 158). Visiting is not the same as *parochialism,* which is not to visit at all but to stay at home. Visiting is also different from *tourism,* which is "to ensure that you will have all the comforts of home even as you travel" (ibid., pp. 158–159). Visiting should, however, also be distinguished from *empathy,* which, as a form of "assimilationism," is "forcibly to make yourself at home in a place that is not your home by appropriating its customs" (ibid., p. 159).

The problem with tourism and empathy is that they both tend to erase plurality. The former does so "by an objectivist stance that holds to 'how we do things' as a lens through which different cultures can only appear as other." The latter trades this spectatorial lens "to assume native glasses, identifying with the new culture so as to avoid the discomfort of being in an unfamiliar place" (ibid.). Visiting, in contrast, is "being and thinking in my own identity where actually I am not" (Arendt 1977c, p. 241). It is to think one's *own* thoughts but in a story very different from one's own, thereby permitting yourself the "disorientation that is necessary to understanding just how the world looks different to someone else" (Disch 1994, p. 159).

The innovative character of the idea of visiting, so I wish to argue, does not lie in the fact that visiting differs from tourism. It is clear that any approach to political judgment that doesn't want to erase plurality has to engage itself with others and otherness. It cannot stay safely at home, neither physically nor virtually, in the sense in which the tourist never comes into unfamiliar places since he always already knows what he will find at the end of his journey. The innovating character of visiting lies in the fact that it provides an alternative for *empathy*. To my mind the main problem with empathy is that it assumes that we can simply (and comfortably) take the position of the other, thereby denying both the situatedness of one's own seeing and thinking and that of the other's. Visiting is therefore *not* to see through the eyes of someone else but to see *with your own eyes* from a position that is *not* your own—or, to be more precise, in a story very different from one's own.

To exist politically thus requires judgment in the way outlined above, and it is this conception of judgment that lies at the heart of the idea of understanding. But rather than to think of understanding as a "capacity" that makes political existence possible, it is more precise to say that understanding as living "with other people, strangers, forever, in the same world" (Arendt 1994, p. 322), *is* existing politically. As Hansen concludes, the "understanding heart, which appears to combine reason and emotion, results not from a fusion of individual wills, a kind of fraternity, but the preservation of a certain sort of distance that yet requires and makes possible worldly ties between people" (Hansen 2005, p. 6). To exist politically is therefore not based upon "fraternity"—upon a common identity or common nature—but upon the preservation of distance and strangeness that only makes worldly ties possible. Existing politically, to put it differently, is not about a common *ground* but about a common *world* (see Gordon 2002). If there is any relationship between political existence and morality in this, it is *not* that morality can guarantee or form the foundation of political existence. At most, it is political existence that makes morality possible (see also Hansen 2005, p. 11). This, in turn, means that the foundation of politics is itself political. Political existence, so we might therefore say, is motivated by nothing but a desire for the space where freedom can appear.

CONCLUSIONS

If we return to the question as to when a child might be "ready" for political existence, we can now give two answers. The first is that a child is *never* ready for political existence for the simple reason that political existence is not based on any particular readiness. This is partly a philosophical point: Arendt's notions of understanding, judgment, bearing with strangers, and trying to be at home in the world are not things that we have to learn (or, for that matter, can learn) so that we can exist politically; they rather describe what existing politically *means*. But we can also look at it empirically and can see that no matter how much children learn to be tolerant and respectful, whether they can actually bear with strangers, whether they are actually able to act in plurality, is always an open question depending on the particularities of the situation. In this regard we might say that whereas children can never be ready for political existence, they also always have to be ready for it. Political existence, bearing with strangers, is not something we can simply postpone when it is not convenient for us.

But while this suggests that we cannot learn *for* political existence, this does not mean that we cannot learn *from* it—and this distinction is, in my view, very important because it allows for a different way to connect education and democratic politics than in terms of preparation and developmentalism. To exist politically, to act "in concert" without erasing plurality, is hard "work" (in the non-Arendtian sense of the word), also because each situation is in some respect unique—so that in each situation we need to some extent to reinvent what political existence might mean, how we can bear plurality and difference, and how we can continue trying to be at home in the world. This will definitely affect our desire for political existence, either positively or negatively. What is unique about schools is the possibility to insert processes of reflection into attempts to exist politically. This is not so much because of a particular authority of educators—although this plays a role too—but first and foremost for the more mundane reason that in school settings children and young people are to a certain extent (and *only* to a certain extent) a "captive audience." This shows what the problem is if we were to declare the school a "no-go area" for political existence, that is, if we were to conceive of the school only as a place for the acquisition of knowledge and skills but not also as a place where freedom might appear, because in that case any learning that might be significant for political existence becomes sterile and disconnected from real experience. It is not only irresponsible to try to keep political existence away from the school; it is also impossible to do so, because the lives of children and young people—inside and outside the school—are permeated by questions about togetherness-in-plurality.

There is another side to this coin as well, because if we continue to think of the relationship between education and democracy in terms of preparation, so that once the preparation has finished democracy can begin, we also take away the opportunities for learning from political existence in the "adult" world (on this see also Biesta 2011b). We deny, in other words, the experimental character of political existence, the fact that political existence can never be guaranteed but always has to be reinvented. We deny, in other words, the weak character of political existence. In a sense, to take away the educational dimension from political existence is even more of a problem than to take away the political dimension from schools, because unlike schools, society doesn't have an apparatus that can "insert" reflection and learning into political existence. This is not to say that no one carries any responsibility for this. It rather is a collective responsibility, a responsibility of "society" (again, not in the Arendtian sense) to keep political existence open toward the future. After all, if we are no longer willing to learn from our political existence but expect that political existence will simply happen, we might as well say that we are no longer trying to be at home in the world, and in this way we have given up the hope that political existence—which for Arendt is ultimately also human existence—is possible at all.

What we need to overcome in order to utilize Arendt's rich and challenging insights into the nature of politics and political existence, therefore, is her "developmentalism," that is, her view that children need special attention and special measures because they are fundamentally different from adults. If there is anything that needs our special attention it is the question of political existence and existing politically itself, both for children and for adults. If there is anything that needs our attention as educators, it will have to be a concern for opportunities to exist politically, a concern for trying to be at home in the world and bear with strangers. This is at the very same time an educational and a political responsibility because what is at stake is the very possibility of our human existence in a common world.

CHAPTER SEVEN

Virtuosity

To know psychology ... is absolutely no guarantee that we shall be good teachers.

—*William James*

In the final chapter of this book I return to the theme of teaching and the teacher, which, in a sense, can be seen as the main thread running through the chapters so far, in that they all try to articulate an understanding of education that is not just about learning but that always returns to questions of teaching and being taught. What I have not spelled out so far is what this actually requires from the teacher, and in this chapter I want to look at this question in more detail. I do this through the angle of teacher education, since much interest in the question as to what teachers should be and should be able to do has arisen in the context of questions about the education of teachers. There are two prominent discourses in relation to this: one, partly coming from policy makers and partly from the educational research community, focuses on the need for teaching to become evidence-based; the other, perhaps more driven through policy, focuses on the idea of competence. While both approaches are not without reason and while they appeal, at least in a rhetorical manner, to a certain "common sense"—after all, who would want to argue that teaching should not make use of research evidence, and who would want to argue that teachers should not be competent?—they are not without problems.

One important problem with the discourse on evidence is that it tends to focus on facts rather than values, and thus has difficulty capturing the insight that education is always framed by purposes and thus by ideas about what good or desirable education is. Also, much of the research that claims to generate evidence on education is biased toward seeing education in "strong" terms, in that it tends to look for causal connections between educational "inputs" and "outcomes" and seems to forget that any connections between teaching and what it effects are weak connections, connections established through interpretation rather than through causation. Third, there is a strong tendency in the discussion about the role of evidence in education to suggest that such evidence should actually replace and overrule professional judgment, thus leading to a disempowerment of teachers and veering toward a culture of educational positivism.

The discourse on teacher competencies is, in this regard, more open and better able to acknowledge the crucial role of the teacher in all educational processes. What is problematic about at least some of the ways in which the notion of competence has been picked up, however, is that it tries to cover for all possible educational eventualities, thus leading to ridiculously long check-lists of everything teachers should be competent in and again forgetting the role of judgment. Also, the ambition to cover all aspects of teaching focuses the competencies discourse strongly on the past—trying to cater for everything that we know so far about what might happen and might be relevant in educational settings—thus making it far less open toward the future. That is why, in this chapter, I make a case for a different approach to the question of teaching and the question of teacher education, one that highlights the crucial role of judgment in always new, open, and unpredictable situations. For reasons I will explain in more detail below, I refer to this approach as a *virtue-based* conception of teaching and teacher education, one that focuses on educational wisdom and the ways in which, through teacher education, we can help teachers to become educationally wise. Thus I suggest that the formation of educational "virtuosity" should be at the heart of teacher education.

The Fear of Being Left Behind

In recent years policy makers and politicians have become increasingly interested in teacher education. In the UK the government has recently published a new policy framework for school education in England—a paper with the interesting title "The Importance of Teaching"[1]—which not only sets out the

---

1. www.education.gov.uk/b0068570/the-importance-of-teaching/ (last accessed August 2, 2012).

parameters for a significant transformation of state-funded school education but also contains specific proposals for the education of teachers. In Scotland the government has recently commissioned a review of Scottish teacher education. This report, with the title "Teaching Scotland's Future,"[2] also makes very specific recommendations about teacher education and about the further professional development of teachers. In addition, discussions about teacher education are increasingly being influenced by developments at the European level, particularly in the context of the Lisbon Strategy, which, in 2000, set the aim of making the European Union into "the most competitive and dynamic knowledge-based economy in the world,"[3] and the Bologna Process, aimed at the creation of a European Higher Education Area, a process that was inaugurated in 1999. In the wake of the 2005 OECD report on the state of teacher education—a report called *Teachers Matter: Attracting, Developing, and Retaining Effective Teachers*[4]—the European Commission produced a document in 2007 called *Improving the Quality of Teacher Education,*[5] which proposed "shared reflection about actions that can be taken at Member State level and how the European Union might support these." As part of this process the European Commission also produced a set of "Common European Principles for Teacher Competences and Qualifications."[6] While none of these documents have any legal power in themselves, they do tend to exert a strong influence on policy development within the member states of the European Union—a point to which I will return below.

One could see the attention from policy makers and politicians to teacher education as a good thing. One could see it as the expression of a real concern for the quality of education at all levels and as recognition of the fact that the quality of teacher education is an important element in the overall picture. But one could also read it more negatively by observing that now that governments in many countries have established a strong grip on schools through a combination of curriculum prescription, testing, inspection, measurement, and league tables, they are now turning their attention to teacher education in order to establish total control over the educational system. Much, of course,

---

2. www.reviewofteachereducationinscotland.org.uk/teachingscotlandsfuture/index.asp (last accessed August 2, 2012).

3. www.consilium.europa.eu/uedocs/cms_data/docs/pressdata/en/ec/00100-r1.en0.htm (last accessed August 2, 2012).

4. www.oecd.org/education/preschoolandschool/48627229.pdf (last accessed August 2, 2012).

5. ec.europa.eu/education/com392_en.pdf (last accessed August 2, 2012).

6. ec.europa.eu/education/policies/2010/doc/principles_en.pdf (last accessed August 2, 2012).

depends on how, in concrete situations, discourse and policy will unfold or have unfolded already. In this regard it is interesting, for example, that whereas in the English situation teaching is being depicted as a *skill* that can be picked up in practice (with the implication that teacher education can be shifted from universities to training schools), the Scottish discussion positions teaching as a *profession,* which, for that very reason, requires proper teacher education, both with regard to teacher preparation and with regard to further professional development. While there are, therefore, still important differences "on the ground," we are, at the very same time, seeing an increasing *convergence* in discourse and policy with regard to teaching—which, in turn, is leading to a convergence in discourse and policy with regard to teacher education. The main concept that seems to be emerging in all of this is the notion of *competence* (see, for example, Deakin Crick 2008; Mulder, Weigel, and Collins 2007).

Competence is an interesting notion for at least two reasons. First, as mentioned, the notion of competence has a certain rhetorical appeal—after all, who would want to argue that teachers should *not* be competent? Second, the idea of competence focuses the discussion on what teachers should be able to *do* rather than only paying attention to what teachers need to *know.* One could say, therefore, that the idea of competence is more practical and, in a sense, also more holistic in that it seems to encompass knowledge, skills, and action as an integrated whole, rather than to see action as, say, the application of knowledge or the implementation of skills. Whether this is indeed so also depends on the particular approach to and conception of competence one favors. Mulder, Weigel, and Collins (2007) show, for example, that within the literature on competence there are three distinctive traditions—the behaviorist, the generic, and the cognitive—that put different emphases on the "mix" between action, cognition, and values. While some definitions of competence are very brief and succinct—such as Eraut's definition of competence as "the ability to perform the tasks and roles required to the expected standards" (Eraut 2003, p. 117, cited in Mulder, Weigel, and Collins 2007)—other definitions, such as, for example, Deakin Crick's definition of competence as "a complex combination of knowledge, skills, understanding, values, attitudes and desire which lead to effective, embodied human action in the world, in a particular domain" (Deakin Crick 2008, p. 313), become so broad that it may be difficult to see what is not included in the idea of competence.

What is worrying, therefore, is perhaps not so much the notion of competence itself—it is a notion with a certain appeal and some potential—but first and foremost the fact that the idea of competence is beginning to monopolize the discourse about teaching and teacher education. It is, therefore, first of all the convergence toward one particular way of thinking and talking about teaching and teacher education that we should be worried about. After all, if there is no alternative discourse, if a particular idea is simply seen as "common sense," then there is a risk that it stops people from thinking at all. While, as mentioned, European documents about teaching and teacher education have no *legal* power—decisions about education remain firmly located at the level of the member states—they do have important *symbolic* and *rhetorical* power in that they often become a reference point that many want to orientate themselves toward, perhaps on the assumption that if they don't adjust themselves to it, they run the risk of being left behind. We can see a similar logic at work in the problematic impact that PISA (the OECD's Programme for International Student Assessment) has had on education in many countries around the world. What I have in mind here is not the fact that PISA is only interested in particular "outcomes"—although there are important questions to be asked about that as well—but first of all the fact that PISA and similar systems create the illusion that a wide range of different educational practices *is* comparable and that, by implication, these practices therefore *ought to* be comparable. Out of a fear of being left behind, out of a fear of ending up at the bottom end of the league table, we can see schools and school systems transforming themselves into the definition of education that "counts" in systems like PISA, the result of it being that more and more schools and school systems begin to become the same.

This, then, is what can happen when a particular discourse becomes hegemonic—that is, when a particular discourse begins to monopolize thinking and talking. It is not so much that the discourse has the power to change everything but rather that people begin to adjust their ways of doing and talking to such ideas. This then generates increased uniformity or, to put it from the other side, a reduction of diversity in educational thought and practice. The argument from biodiversity shows what is dangerous about such a development, as a reduction of diversity erodes the ability of a system to respond effectively and creatively to changes in the environment. Also, the fact that the move toward uniformity is more often than not driven by fear, that is, driven by a lack of courage to think and act differently and independently, makes such developments even more worrying, as we all know that fear is not a very good counselor.

But it is not only the tendency toward uniformity that is problematic here. It is also that through the discourse about competence, about the competent teacher and about the competencies that teacher education should develop in teachers, that a very particular view about education is being repeated, promoted, and *multiplied*. This is often not how ideas about the competences that teachers need are being presented. Such competences are often presented as general, as relatively open to different views about education, as relatively neutral with regard to such views, and also as relatively uncontested. They are, in other words, presented as "common sense." One thing that is important, therefore, is to open up this common sense by showing that it is possible to think *differently* about education and about what teachers should be able to do, at least in order to move away from an unreflected and unreflective common sense about education. But I also wish to argue that the particular common sense about education that is being multiplied is problematic in itself, because it has a tendency to promote what I would see as a rather un-educational way of thinking about education. And this is the deeper problem that needs to be addressed in order to have a better starting point for the discussion about teacher education.

THE "LEARNIFICATION" OF EDUCATION

There are a number of places where I could start, but by way of example I will use the key competences enlisted in the document from the Directorate-General for Education and Culture of the European Commission, called "Common European Principles for Teacher Competences and Qualifications."

MAKING IT WORK: THE KEY COMPETENCES

Teaching and education add to the economic and cultural aspects of the knowledge society and should therefore be seen in their societal context. Teachers should be able to:

Work with others: they work in a profession which should be based on the values of social inclusion and nurturing the potential of every learner. They need to have knowledge of human growth and development and demonstrate self-confidence when engaging with others. They need to be able to work with learners as individuals and support them to develop into fully participating and active members of society. They should also be able to work in ways which increase the collective intelligence of learners and co-operate and collaborate with colleagues to enhance their own learning and teaching.

Work with knowledge, technology and information: they need to be able to work with a variety of types of knowledge. Their education and professional development should equip them to access, analyse, validate, reflect on and transmit knowledge, making effective use of technology where this is appropriate. Their pedagogic skills should allow them to build and manage learning environments and retain the intellectual freedom to make choices over the delivery of education. Their confidence in the use of ICT should allow them to integrate it effectively into learning and teaching. They should be able to guide and support learners in the networks in which information can be found and built. They should have a good understanding of subject knowledge and view learning as a lifelong journey. Their practical and theoretical skills should also allow them to learn from their own experiences and match a wide range of teaching and learning strategies to the needs of learners.

Work with and in society: they contribute to preparing learners to be globally responsible in their role as EU citizens. Teachers should be able to promote mobility and co-operation in Europe, and encourage intercultural respect and understanding. They should have an understanding of the balance between respecting and being aware of the diversity of learners' cultures and identifying common values. They also need to understand the factors that create social cohesion and exclusion in society and be aware of the ethical dimensions of the knowledge society. They should be able to work effectively with the local community, and with partners and stakeholders in education—parents, teacher education institutions, and representative groups. Their experience and expertise should also enable them to contribute to systems of quality assurance. Teachers' work in all these areas should be embedded in a professional continuum of lifelong learning which includes initial teacher education, induction and continuing professional development, as they cannot be expected to possess all the necessary competences on completing their initial teacher education.[7]

There is, of course, a lot that can be said about this text, and I would say that documents like these do require careful and detailed critical analysis. For the purpose of this chapter I would like to make two observations. The first is that in this text, school-education is very much positioned as an instrument that needs to deliver all kinds of societal goods. Education needs to produce such things as social cohesion, social inclusion, a knowledge society, lifelong learning, a knowledge economy, EU citizens, intercultural respect and understanding, a sense of common values, and so on. In terms of its agenda this is a very

---

7. From http://ec.europa.eu/education/policies/2010/doc/principles_en.pdf (last accessed August 2, 2012).

functionalist view of education and a very functionalist view of what is core to what teachers need to be able to do. It paints a picture where society—and there is of course always the question who "society" actually "is"—sets the agenda, and where education is seen as an instrument for the delivery of this agenda. Also, in this text the only "intellectual freedom" granted to teachers is about *how* to "deliver" this agenda, not about what it is that is supposed to be "delivered." (I put "delivery" in quotation marks to highlight that it is a very unfortunate and unhelpful metaphor to talk about education in the first place.) This functionalist or instrumentalist view of education does not seem to consider the idea that education may have other interests, but predominantly thinks of the school as the institution that needs to solve "other people's problems," to put it briefly.

My second observation concerns the fact that in this text, education is predominantly described in terms of *learning*. We read that teachers are supposed to nurture the potential of every learner, that they need to be able to work with learners as individuals, that they should aim at increasing the collective intelligence of learners, that they should be able to build and manage learning environments, integrate ICT effectively into learning and teaching, provide guidance and support to learners in information networks, and view learning as a lifelong journey. For me this document is therefore another example of what I have referred to in earlier chapters as the rise of a "new language of learning" in education and the wider "learnification" of educational discourse. This rise, as discussed, is manifest in a number of "translations" that have taken place in the language used in educational practice, educational policy, and educational research. We can see it in the tendency to refer to students, pupils, children, and even adults as learners. We can see it in the tendency to refer to teaching as the facilitation of learning or the management of learning environments. We can see it in the tendency to refer to schools as places for learning or as learning environments. And we can see it in the tendency no longer to speak about adult education but rather to talk about lifelong learning.

Perhaps the quickest way to highlight the problem here is to say that the purpose of education is *not* that children and students learn, but that they learn *something* and that they do so for particular reasons and with reference to particular purposes. A major problem with the language of learning, as I have argued, is that it is a language of *process*, but not a language of content and purpose. Yet education is never just about learning, but is always about the learning of something for particular purposes. Also, whereas the language of learning is an *individualistic* language—learning is after all something you can do on your own—the language of education is a *relational* language, where there is always the idea of someone educating somebody else. The problem with the rise of the language of learning in education is therefore threefold: it is a language that makes it more difficult to ask questions about content; it is a language that makes it more difficult to ask questions of purpose; and it is a language that makes it more difficult to ask questions about the specific role and responsibility of the teacher in the educational relationship.

While, as mentioned, the idea of competence is therefore, in itself, not necessarily bad, I am concerned about the way in which it is multiplying a particular view about education through a particular language about education, the language of learning. This means that if we wish to say anything *educational* about teacher education, if, in other words, we wish to move beyond the language of learning, we need to engage with a way of speaking and thinking that is more properly educational. Once we do this we may find—and this is what I will be arguing below—that the idea of competences becomes less attractive and less appropriate to think about teacher education and its future. Let me move, then, to the next step in my argument, which has to do with the nature of educational practices.

WHAT IS EDUCATION FOR?

Let me begin with a brief anecdote. Until recently experienced teachers in Scotland had the opportunity to follow a specially designed master's program in order to obtain a higher qualification. Teachers who have successfully gone through this program can call themselves "chartered teachers" (just like, for example, chartered accountants or chartered surveyors). One of the things that the teachers studying on this program need to be able to do is show that through the conduct of small-scale inquiry projects they can *improve* their practice. What I found remarkable in working with students on this program is that while most of them were able to provide evidence about the fact that they had been able to *change* their practice, they found it quite difficult to articulate why such changes would count as an *improvement* of their practice. Quite often they thought, at least initially, that a change in practice is automatically an improvement, until I suggested that each time a practice has changed we can still ask the question why such change is an improvement, that is, why that change is *desirable* change, why the changed situation is *better* than what existed before. There is only one way in which we can answer this question, and that is through engagement with the question of what education is *for*, that is, the question about the purpose of education. It is, after all, only if we are able to articulate what it is we want to achieve, that we can judge whether a change in practice gets us closer to this or further away from it.

By arguing that there is a need to engage with the question of educational purpose, I am not trying to define what the purpose of education should be. But I do wish to make two points about how I think we should engage with the question of purpose. The first point is that educational practices, in my view, always serve more than one purpose—and do so at the very same time. The *multidimensionality of educational purpose* is precisely what makes education interesting. It is also (and this is my second point, to which I will return below) the reason why a particular kind of judgment is needed in education. By saying that that question of educational purpose is multidimensional, I am suggesting that education "functions" or "works" in a number of different dimensions and that in each of these dimensions the question of purpose needs to be raised. As I have already mentioned in previous chapters, I have in several of my publications suggested that educational processes and practices tend to function in three different domains and that with regard to each domain we need to raise the question of purpose (see Biesta 2010b; see also Biesta 2009). I have referred to these domains as *qualification, socialization,* and *subjectification. Qualification* roughly has to do with the ways in which education qualifies people for doing things—in the broad sense of the word—by equipping them with knowledge, skills, and dispositions. This is a very important dimension of school education, and some would even argue that it is the only thing that should matter in schools. Education is, however, not only about knowledge, skills, and dispositions but also has to do with the ways in which, through education, we become part of existing social, cultural, and political practices and traditions. This is the *socialization* dimension of education, where, to put it in more general terms, the orientation is on the "insertion" of newcomers into existing orders. Newcomers, here, can be both children and those who move from one country or one culture to another. We can also think here of the ways in which education introduces newcomers into particular professional orders and cultures. While some, as mentioned, take a very strict and narrow view of education and would argue that the only task of schools is to be concerned about knowledge and skills and dispositions, we can see that over the past decades the socialization function has become an explicit dimension of discussions about what schools are for. We can see this specifically in the range of societal "agendas" that have been added to the school curriculum, such as environmental education, citizenship education, social and moral education, sex education, and so on. The idea here is that education not only exerts a socializing force on children and students, but that it is actually desirable that education should do this.

Now while, again, some people would argue that these are the only two proper and legitimate dimensions that school education should be concerned about, I have argued that there is a third dimension in which education operates and should operate. This has to do with the way in which education impacts the person, which is the dimension of *subjectification*. It is important to see that subjectification and socialization are not the same—and one of the important challenges for contemporary education is how we can actually articulate the distinction between the two (for more on this see Biesta 2006a). Socialization has to do with how we become part of existing orders, how we identify with such orders and thus obtain an identity; subjectification, in contrast, is always about how we can exist "outside" of such orders, so to speak. With a relatively "old" but still crucially important concept, we can say that subjectification has to do with the question of human freedom—which, of course, then raises further questions about how we should understand human freedom.

To engage with the question of purpose in education, so I wish to suggest, requires that we engage with this question in relation to all three domains. It requires that we think about what we aim to achieve in relation to qualification, socialization, and subjectification. The reason why engagement with the question of purpose requires that we "cover" all three domains lies in the fact that anything we do in education potentially has "impact" in any of these three domains. It is important to acknowledge that the three domains are *not separate,* which is why I tend to depict them through a Venn diagram of three overlapping areas. The overlap is important because on the one hand this indicates opportunities for *synergy,* whereas on the other hand it can also help us to see potential *conflict* between the different dimensions. An example of potential synergy is the way in which in vocational education the teaching of particular skills at the same time functions as a way to socialize students into particular domains of work, into professional responsibility and the like. An example of potential conflict is that where a constant pressure on testing and exams, which is perhaps an effective way to drive up achievement in the domain of qualification, can have a negative impact on the domain of subjectification if it teaches students that competition is always better than cooperation.

Given the possibility of synergy and of conflict, and given the fact that our educational activities almost always "work" in the three domains at the very same time, looking at education through these dimensions begins to make visible something that in my view is absolutely central about the work of teachers, which is the need for making situated judgments about what is educationally desirable in relation to these three dimensions. What is central to the work of teachers is not simply that they set aims and implement them. Because education is multidimensional, teachers constantly need to make judgments about how to balance the different dimensions; they need to set priorities—which can never be set in general but always need to be set in concrete situations with regard to concrete students—and they need to be able to handle tensions and conflicts and should be able to see and utilize possibilities for synergy. All this is at play in this simple distinction between "change" and "improvement." Answering the question whether change is improvement is, therefore, not only a matter of assessing progress toward one particular aim. Because of the multidimensionality of education we always need to consider the possibility that gain with regard to one dimension may be loss with regard to another.

What is beginning to emerge from this line of thinking is the suggestion that because the question of the aim or "telos" of education is a multidimensional question, judgment—judgment about what is educationally *desirable*—turns out to be an absolutely crucial element of what teachers do.

JUDGMENT AND WISDOM IN EDUCATION

If I try to bring the lines of my argument so far together, the point that is emerging is that the question is not so much whether teachers should be competent to do things—one could say that of course they should be competent—but that competence, the ability to do things, is in itself *never enough*. To put it bluntly: a teacher who possesses all the competences teachers need but who is unable to judge which competence needs to be deployed when, is a useless teacher. Judgments about what needs to be done always need to be made with reference to the purposes of education—which is why the language of learning is unhelpful as it is not a language in which the question of purpose can easily be raised, articulated, and addressed. And since the question of purpose of education is a multidimensional question, the judgment that is needed needs to be *multidimensional*, taking into consideration that a gain with regard to one dimension may be a loss with regard to another dimension—so that there is a need to make judgment about the right *balance* and the right *trade-off* between gains and losses, so to speak. Exerting such judgments is not something that is done at the level of school policy documents, but lies at the very heart of what goes on in the classroom and in the relationships between teachers and students—and this goes on again, and again, and again.

While some might argue that this is an argument for saying that teachers need to be competent in making educational judgments, I would rather want to see the capacity for judgment as something different from competences. Part of my argument for this is that if we would see the ability for educational judgments as a competence, it would be the one and only competence on the list. But we could also say that to the extent that there is something reasonable in the idea that teachers should be competent in doing certain things, there is always the further need to judge when it is appropriate to do what.

A similar argument for the absolutely central role of educational judgments can be made in relation to another tendency we can find in discussions about teaching and teacher education, which is the idea that teaching should develop into an evidence-based profession just as, for example, people have argued that medicine should develop into an evidence-based profession. This is a big and complicated discussion, which I have explored in much more critical detail elsewhere (see Biesta 2007b, 2010c, 2010d). The main point for this chapter is whether it is a good idea that rather than for education to rely on the judgment of professionals it should be based on strong scientific evidence about "what works." The idea is that such evidence can be generated through large-scale experimental studies where there is an experimental group who gets a particular "treatment" and a control group who doesn't get this "treatment," in order then to measure whether the "treatment" had any particular effect. If it did, then—so the argument goes—we have evidence that the treatment "works" and therefore have an evidence base that tells us what to do.

Even if, for the sake of the argument, we would concede that it might be possible to conduct the kind of studies suggested above, the outcomes of those studies are limited in two ways. One point is that such studies at most give us knowledge about *the past*. That is, they give us knowledge about what may have worked in the past, but there is no guarantee whatsoever—at least not in the domain of human interaction—that what has worked in the past will also work in the future. This already means that such knowledge can at most give us possibilities for action, but not rules. While it may therefore have the possibility to *inform* our judgments, it cannot *replace* our judgments about what needs to be done. And judgment is also important because something that may work in relation to one dimension of education may actually have a detrimental effect in relation to another dimension.

So just as competences in themselves are not enough to capture what teaching is about, the idea of education as an evidence-based profession makes even less sense. What is missing in both cases is the absolutely crucial role of educational judgment. Particularly with regard to the latter discussion—that is, about the role of scientific evidence—this brings us back to a question that has been circulating in discussions about education for a fairly long time, which is the question whether teaching is an art or a science. One person who has very concisely and very convincingly argued against the idea of teaching as a science is William James (1842–1910). In his *Talks to Teachers on Psychology* (James 1899) he formulated his position as follows.

Psychology is a science, and teaching is an art; and sciences never generate arts directly out of themselves. An intermediary inventive mind must make the application, by using its originality.

The most such sciences can do is to help us to catch ourselves up and check ourselves, if we start to reason or to behave wrongly; and to criticize ourselves more articulately after we have made mistakes.

To know psychology, therefore, is absolutely no guarantee that we shall be good teachers. To advance to that result, we must have an additional endowment altogether, a happy tact and ingenuity to tell us what definite things to say and do when the pupil is before us. That ingenuity in meeting and pursuing the pupil, that tact for the concrete situation, though they are the alpha and omega of the teacher's art, are things to which psychology cannot help us in the least. (James 1899, pp. 14–15)

While James provides a convincing argument why teaching should not and cannot be understood as a science—and actually needs tact, ingenuity, and, so I wish to add, judgment—James has less to say about the positive side of the argument, that is, the idea that education should therefore be understood as an art. It is here that I turn to Aristotle, not only because he has interesting things to say about this question but perhaps more importantly because he helps us to move beyond the question whether teaching is a science or an art and toward the question of *what kind of an art* teaching actually is.

Aristotle's argument starts from the distinction between the theoretical life and the practical life. While the theoretical life has to do with "the necessary and the eternal" (Aristotle 1980, p. 140) and thus with a kind of knowledge to which Aristotle refers as science (*episteme*), the practical life has to do with what is "variable" (ibid., p. 142), that is, with the world of change. This is the world in which we act and in which our actions make a difference. With regard to our operations in the world of change Aristotle makes a distinction between two modes of acting, *poiesis* and *praxis*, or, in Carr's (1987) translation, "making action" and "doing action." Both modes of action require judgment, but the kind of judgment needed is radically different, and this is an important insight for the art of education. *Poiesis* is about the production or fabrication of things—such as, for example, a saddle or a ship. It is, as Aristotle puts it, about "how something may come into being which is capable of either being or not being" (which means that it is about the variable, not about what is eternal and necessary), and about things "whose origin is in the maker and not in the thing made" (which distinguishes *poiesis* from biological phenomena such as growth and development) (see Aristotle 1980, p. 141). *Poiesis* is, in short, about the creation of something that did not exist before. The kind of knowledge we need for *poiesis* is *techne* (usually translated as "art"). It is, in more contemporary vocabulary, technological or instrumental knowledge, "knowledge of how to make things" (ibid., p. 141). Aristotle comments that *poiesis* "has an end other than itself" (ibid., p. 143). The end of *poiesis* is *external* to the means, which means that *techne,* the knowledge of how to make things, is about finding the means that will produce the thing one wants to make. *Techne* therefore encompasses knowledge about the materials we work with and about the techniques we can apply to work with those materials. But making a saddle is never about simply following a recipe. It involves making judgments about the application of our general knowledge to *this* piece of leather, for *this* horse, and for *this* person riding the horse. So we make judgments about application, production, and effectiveness as our focus is on producing something—or, to be more precise, producing some *thing*.

However, the domain of the variable is not confined to the world of things but also includes the social world—the world of human action and interaction. This is the domain of *praxis.* The orientation here, as Aristotle puts it, is not toward the production of things but to bringing about "goodness" or human flourishing (*eudamonia*). *Praxis* is "about what sort of things conduce to the good life in general" (ibid., p. 142). It is about good action, but good action is not a means for the achievement of something else. "Good action itself is its end" (ibid., p. 143). The kind of judgment we need here is not about *how* things should be done; we need judgment "about *what is to be done*" (ibid.; emphasis added). Aristotle refers to this kind of judgment as *phronesis,* which is usually translated as "practical wisdom." Phronesis is a "reasoned and true state of capacity to act with regard to human goods" (ibid., p. 143).

Two points follow from this. The first has to do with the nature of education, where I would argue, with Aristotle, that we should never think of education *only* as a process of production, that is, of *poiesis.* While education is clearly located in the domain of the variable, it is concerned with the interaction between human beings, not the interaction between human beings and the material world. Education, in other words, is a social art, and the aesthetics of the social is in important ways different from the aesthetics of the material (which is not to say that they are entirely separate). This does not mean that we should exclude the idea of *poiesis* from our educational thinking. After all, we do want our teaching and our curricula to have effect and be effective; we do want our students to become good citizens, skillful professionals, knowledgeable human beings; and for that we do need to think about educational processes in terms of *poiesis,* that is, in terms of bringing about some*thing*. But that should never be the be-all and end-all of education. Education is always more than just production, than just *poiesis,* and—as I have argued throughout the chapters in this book—ultimately education is precisely what production/ *poiesis* is *not*, because at the end of the day we, as educators, cannot claim and should not want to claim that we produce our students. We educate them, and we educate them *in* freedom and *for* freedom. That is why what matters in education—what makes education educational—does not lie in the domain of *poiesis* but in the domain of *praxis*. It shows, in other words, why education is ultimately a social art and not a material art (and this can be seen as another reason why the whole approach emanating from discussions about evidence-based practice is misplaced where it concerns education).

The second point I wish to make is that practical wisdom, the kind of wisdom we need in relation to *praxis* with the intention to bring about goodness, captures quite well what I have been saying about educational judgment. Educational judgments are, after all, judgments about what needs to be done, not with the aim to produce something in the technical sense but with the aim to bring about what is considered to be educationally desirable (in the three—overlapping—domains I have identified). Such judgments are, therefore, not technical judgments but are value judgments. What Aristotle adds to the picture—and this is important for developing these views about education into views about teacher education—is that practical wisdom is not to be understood as a set of skills or dispositions or a set of competences, but rather denotes a certain quality or excellence of the person. The Greek term here is ἀρετή, and the English translation of ἀρετή is *virtue*. The ability to make wise educational judgments should therefore not be seen as some kind of "add on," that is, something that does not affect us as a person, but rather denotes what we might call a holistic quality, something that permeates and characterizes the whole person—and we can take "characterize" here quite literally, as virtue is often also translated as "character."

The question is therefore not how we can learn *phronesis*. The question rather is, How can we become a *phronimos*? How can we become a practically wise *person*? And more specifically the question is, How can we become an *educationally wise person*? Now this, so I wish to suggest, is the question of teacher education.

Becoming Educationally Wise

How might we become educationally wise? With regard to this question Aristotle makes a further interesting point when he writes "that a young man of practical wisdom cannot be found" (ibid., p. 148). What he is saying here is that wisdom is something that comes with age—or perhaps it's better to say that wisdom comes with *experience*, and this provides an important pointer for the question of teacher education. What is also relevant is the fact that each time Aristotle comes to the point where one would expect to get a definition of what a practically wise person looks like, he doesn't provide an abstract description of certain traits and qualities but rather comes with actual examples of people who exemplify practical wisdom—such as, in the case of statesmanship, Pericles. It is as if Aristotle is saying, if you want to know what practical wisdom is, if you want to know what a practically wise person looks like, look at him, look at her, because they are excellent examples and examples of excellence. So how might this help us in reframing teacher education if it focuses on the question of how one might become educationally wise?

The first implication is that teacher education should be concerned with the *formation of the whole person* (not, so I wish to emphasize, as a private individual but as a professional). This is partly a matter of professional socialization but certainly also carries aspects of what we might call professional subjectification. Teacher education is not just about the acquisition of knowledge, skills, and dispositions (qualification) or just about doing as other teachers do (socialization) but starts from the formation and transformation of the person, and it is only from there that questions about knowledge, skills, and dispositions, about values and traditions, about competence and evidence come in, so to speak. The guiding principle here is the idea of educational wisdom, that is, the ability to make wise educational judgments. Following Aristotle, we can call this a virtue-based approach to teaching and a virtue-based approach to teacher education. While we could say that what we are after here is for teacher students to become virtuous professionals, I prefer to play differently with the idea of virtue and would like to suggest that what we should be after in teacher education is a kind of *virtuosity* in making wise educational judgments.

The idea of virtuosity can help us to identify two further dimensions of a virtue-based approach to the formation of teachers, because if we think about the way in which musicians develop their virtuosity, we can see that they do so by practicing the very thing they aim to develop their virtuosity in, and by observing and studying the virtuosity of others. This leads us precisely to the other two components of the approach to teacher education I wish to suggest.

The second component, therefore, is the idea that we can develop our virtuosity for wise educational judgment only by *practicing* judgment, that is, by being engaged in making such judgment in the widest range of educational situations possible. It is not, in other words, that we can become good at judgment by reading books about it; we have to do it, and we have to learn from doing it. At one level one might argue that this is not a very original idea, that is, that we can only really learn the art of teaching through doing it. But I do think that there is an important difference between, say, learning on the job (the picking-skills-up-on-the-job approach), or reflective practice, or even problem-based learning. What I am after is what we might call *judgment-based* professional formation, or *judgment-focused* professional formation. It is not just about any kind of experiential or practical learning, but one that constantly takes the ability for making wise educational judgments as its point of reference—which means that it constantly engages with the question as to what is educationally desirable in relation to a particular constellation of educational purposes.

The third component has to do with the role of examples. While on the one hand we can only develop virtuosity through practicing judgment ourselves, there is also much to be gained from studying the virtuosity of others, particularly those who we deem to have reached a certain level of educational virtuosity.[8] This is not to be understood as a process of collaborative learning or peer-learning. The whole idea of studying the virtuosity of others is that you focus on those who exemplify the very thing you aspire to, so to speak. The process is, in other words, asymmetrical rather than symmetrical. The study of the virtuosity of other teachers can take many different forms. It can be done in the classroom through the observation of the ways in which teachers make embodied and situated wise educational judgments—or at least try to do so. We have to bear in mind, though, that such judgments are not always obvious or visible—also because virtuosity is something that becomes embodied over time—so there is also need for conversation, for talking to teachers to find out why they did what they did. This can be done on a small scale—teacher students interviewing teachers about their judgments and their educational virtuosity—but it can also be done on a bigger scale, for example through life-history work with experienced teachers, so that we get a sense not only of their virtuosity but perhaps also of the trajectory through which they have developed their educational virtuosity throughout their career.

---

8. An interesting question here is whether we should only focus on those who exemplify educational virtuosity, or whether we can also gain from studying those who do not exemplify this virtuosity. The more general question here is whether we can learn most from good examples or from bad examples. With regard to educational virtuosity I am inclined to argue that it is only when we have developed a sense of what virtuosity looks like that we can benefit from studying those cases where such virtuosity is absent.

CONCLUSIONS

These, then, are three reference points for teacher education that follow if we do not think of teaching in terms of evidence or competences but rather with a focus on judgment and, more specifically, on educational judgment. Such a capacity for judgment is not to be understood as a skill or competence but rather as a quality that characterizes the whole educational professional—which is the reason why I have referred to this as a virtue-based approach to teaching and to teacher education. The main focus is on the development of a certain virtuosity in making educational judgments—not, again, as a set of skills or competences but rather as a process that will help teachers to become educationally wise. Such wisdom is particularly important in order to capture that our educational actions are never just a repetition of what has happened in the past but are always radically open toward the future. We need judgment rather than recipes in order to be able to engage with this openness and do so in an educational way.

For a Pedagogy of the Event

In the preceding pages I have reflected from a number of angles and through a number of educational "themes" on the weakness of education. I have not only tried to show the weak ways in which education "works" but have also emphasized the crucial importance of the fact that education—or as I have put it in some places, education worthy of the name, that is, education that is not only interested in qualification and socialization but also in subjectification, that is, in the possibility of the event of subjectivity—can only "operate" in weak existential ways and not in strong metaphysical ways. That is why I have argued that we shouldn't understand the "act" of educational creation as that of bringing being into existence—a metaphysical maneuver—but rather that of bringing (or better, calling) being into life. It is why I have highlighted that real educational communication (as distinguished from the transportation of information from A to B) is a radically open and undetermined process and hence a process that is always "in deconstruction"—which, in turn, means that we should refrain from trying to totalize communication through our theoretical understandings of it but should always "risk" those theories themselves by bringing them into communication. It is why I have suggested that the experience of "being taught" cannot be produced by the teacher so that, in this sense, teaching is the giving of a gift the teacher doesn't possess. It is why I have argued for the need to de-naturalize the idea of "learning" so that it ceases to have power over us and can again become something we have power over. It is why I have explored an understanding of emancipation that is not about a powerful intervention in which one person sets another person free so as to bring about equality, but about a process in which emancipation is "seized" by those who start from the assumption of equality. It is why I have argued that democracy is not premised upon a psychological state that can be reached at the end of an appropriate developmental trajectory, but has to be understood as a mode of existence that is orientated toward the appearance of freedom. And it is why I have argued that teaching is not a matter of following recipes but ultimately requires teachers who are able to make wise situated judgments about what is educationally desirable.

In each case there is of course a risk. To engage with the openness and unpredictability of education, to be orientated toward an event that may or may not happen, to take communication seriously, to acknowledge that the power of the teacher is structurally limited, to see that emancipation and democracy cannot be produced in a machine-like manner, and to acknowledge that education can never be reduced to the logic of *poiesis* but always also needs the logic of *phronesis,* means to take this risk seriously, and to do so *not* because the risk is deemed to be inevitable—it is, after all, conceivable that at some point in the future and through a huge effort we may be able to take all unpredictability out of education—but because without the risk, education itself disappears and social reproduction, insertion into existing orders of being, doing, and thinking, takes over. While this may be desirable if our orientation is toward the reproduction of what already exists, it is not desirable if we are genuinely interested in education as a process that has an interest in the coming into the world of free subjects, not in the production of docile objects. For this we do not need a pedagogy of cause and effect, a pedagogy that just aims to generate pre-specified "learning outcomes." We rather need a pedagogy of the *event,* a pedagogy that is orientated positively toward the weakness of education. This is a pedagogy, in short, that is indeed willing to take the beautiful risk of education.

Coming into the World, Uniqueness, and the Beautiful Risk of Education

An Interview with Gert Biesta by Philip Winter

PW: Is there a theory of education in your work?

GB: There probably is, although I have to say that this is more something that has emerged over the years than that it is something that I deliberately set out to develop. While I have always been interested in theoretical and philosophical questions about education, it was probably only when I started to work on my book *Beyond Learning* (Biesta 2006a) that things came together and a theory of education emerged—and even then I was only able to articulate what this theory was about after I had finished the book.

PW: Can you briefly describe what this theory is about and how it "works"?

GB: Sure. Conceptually it hangs on two notions, "coming into the world" and "uniqueness." To understand why those notions are there and why they matter, I probably need to say a few things about the issues I was responding to in developing these ideas. The work on "coming into the world" started in the late 1990s when I was invited to contribute to a conference on identity. When I started to explore that notion I realized a number of things. One was that I was actually not really interested in the question of *identity*—which for me is always the question of identification (identification by someone and/or identification with something) and therefore always articulates a third-person perspective; identity is an explanatory concept, one could say—but much more in the question of *subjectivity,* that is, the question of how we can be or become a subject of action and responsibility. For me that is the educational question, whereas identity is much more a sociological and psychological problematic.

By then I had already read enough of Foucault to understand that, unlike what many people still seem to think, the whole discussion about the death of the subject was not about the death of the very possibility of subjectivity—or "subject-ness"—but rather was aimed at the idea that it is possible to speak the truth about the subject, that is, to claim to know what the subject is and to claim that it is possible to have such knowledge. One can of course treat this entirely as a philosophical matter, but I was interested in how the idea that it is possible to speak the truth about the human subject actually "works," that is, what it is doing and has been doing in a range of domains, including education and politics.

It was at that point that I realized that education—or as I now would say, *modern* education—tends to be based on a truth about the nature and destiny of the human being, a truth about what the child is and what the child must become, to put it in educational terms. Notions such as "autonomy" and "rationality" play an important role in modern educational thought and practice. While I'm all for autonomy and rationality, both notions are not without problems. Is it the case, for example, that we can ever be completely autonomous? What would that actually look like? And isn't it the case that the border between rationality and irrationality is historical and, in a sense, political rather than that it is simply "there" or can be found deep down inside the human being? In addition to these more general and in a sense more philosophical questions, I was also concerned for those who may never be able to achieve autonomy or rationality. Are they beyond the scope of education? Are they outside of the sphere of politics? Are they beyond the scope of what it means to be human? The idea of speaking the truth about the human being was for me, therefore, not just as a philosophical question; for me it was first and foremost an educational, a political, and an existential question. That is why I was less interested in trying to articulate what the subject *is*—which, when I pursued this theme in the writing of philosophers such as Heidegger,

Levinas, Foucault, and Derrida, was an impossibility anyway. I rather tried to find a language that could capture how the subject *exists*.

What I picked up from Jean Luc Nancy was the idea of "coming into presence," which for me was a much more existential way to talk about the subject, one that referred to an *event* rather than an essence or identity, and one that expresses an interest in who comes into presence rather than that it tries to define what is to come, ought to come, or is allowed to come into presence. The idea of "coming into presence" thus turned traditional educational thinking on its head by not starting from what the child is to become, but by articulating an interest in that which announces itself as a new beginning, as newness, as natality, to use Arendt's term. What is crucial about the event of "coming into presence" is that this is not something that can be done in isolation. To come into presence is always to come into the presence of *others*—which led me to an exploration of what one might call the relational dimensions of the event of subjectivity. Some of this was informed by my earlier work on pragmatism and the idea of intersubjectivity, but what I felt was missing from pragmatism was an awareness of what I would now call the deconstructive nature of "coming into presence," that is, the idea that the condition of possibility for anyone's "coming into presence" is at the same time its conditions of impossibility. I drew some inspiration from the work of the Swiss architect Bernhard Tschumi, who at the time was arguing for a conception of architecture that included the way in which people make use of buildings and through this always interrupt the architectural program. But the main inspiration came from Hannah Arendt and her notion of "action."

Arendt not only helped me to see that my coming into presence always depends on how my beginnings are taken up by others. She also helped me to see that if we are committed to a world in which everyone's beginnings can come into presence, we have to live with the fact—which is actually not a fact but an articulation of what it means to exist politically (Biesta 2010e)—that the ways in which others take up my beginnings are radically beyond my control. The very condition that makes my "coming into presence" possible—that is, the fact that others take up my beginnings—also disrupts the purity of my beginnings, so to speak, as others should have the freedom to take up my beginnings in their own ways. Arendt's intriguing phrase "plurality is the condition of human action" still captures this very well, as it is only under the condition of plurality that *everyone's* beginnings can come into presence, and not just the beginnings of one single individual. It is because of this line of thinking that I shifted from the notion of "coming into presence" to the notion of "coming into the world." The main reason for this was to highlight what I see as the inherently political nature of the event of subjectivity, that is, the fact that the event of subjectivity can only happen in a world of plurality and difference—a *polis* or public sphere, so we might say. Educationally all this means that the responsibility of the educator can never only be directed toward individuals—individual children—and their "coming into presence" but also needs to be directed to the maintenance of a space in which, as Arendt puts it, "freedom can appear." It is, therefore, a double responsibility: for the child *and* for the world and, more specifically, for the "worldly" quality of the world.

PW: And what about uniqueness?

GB: The idea of uniqueness is important because if we only were to have the idea of "coming into the world," we would have an account of how the event of subjectivity occurs—we would have a theory of subjectivity, to put it differently—but we would not have an argument for why the subjectivity of each single subject who comes into the world might matter. That is why the idea of "coming into the world" needs to be complemented by a notion of "uniqueness." But there are two ways in which uniqueness can be articulated—one that brings us back to identity and questions about knowledge of the subject, and one that leads us to an existential argument. In my work I have articulated this as the distinction between "uniqueness-as-difference" and "uniqueness-as-irreplaceability" (Biesta 2010b)—and the inspiration for the latter approach comes from Emmanuel Levinas. Uniqueness as difference focuses on our characteristics, on what we *have,* and articulates how each of us is in some respect different from everyone else. Again we could say that this is a third-person perspective, but what is more problematic here is that uniqueness-as-difference is based on an instrumental relationship with the other: we need others in order to articulate that we are different from them, but that's all that we need the other for. Uniqueness-as-irreplaceability, in contrast, brings in a different question: not what *makes* me unique, but *when does it matter* that I am I? The brief answer to this question is that this matters when I am being addressed, when someone appeals to me, when someone calls me. Those are situations in which I am singled out by the other, so to speak. And in those situations—if the other is after *me,* not after me in my social role (which would be my identity)—we are irreplaceable; or to be more precise, we are irreplaceable in our responsibility for the other. Whether we take up this responsibility, whether we take responsibility for our responsibility, to use Zygmunt Bauman's phrase, is entirely up to us. There is no theory that can tell us that we should do this. Nor can the other command that I should take up my responsibility. This is entirely up to me. In this sense, therefore, the idea of uniqueness-as-irreplaceability not only articulates a first-person perspective but is also entirely existential. It claims nothing about what the subject *is*—just about situations we can find ourselves in, situations in which we are literally singled out and in which our uniqueness matters. I still find this quite a powerful way to engage with the event of subjectivity—and also a quite beautiful way, actually. I don't see it as a theory of subjectivity but have rather called it an "ethics of subjectivity" (Biesta 2008)—as the question of subjectivity, of the event of subjectivity, is approached in ethical terms, rather than in epistemological or ontological ones, which is another way of saying that about the human subject there is nothing to know.

PW: How does this relate to "coming into the world"?

GB: Well, in a sense it specifies how uniqueness can come into the world. But uniqueness is an event, not something the individual can possess or claim to possess (or claim to know, for that matter). As an event it is therefore something that always is at stake, where there is always the question whether the event of subjectivity can be achieved—which is perhaps already a bit too active as a term.

PW: What can educators do with these ideas?

GB: Very little, actually—that is, if you take doing in the Aristotelian sense of *poiesis,* that is, to think of doing as production. And there is of course a long tradition in which education is understood along those lines, that is, as a process that needs to produce something, that needs to have certain outcomes, as in the currently all too popular phrase of "learning outcomes." But we do not produce our students; we are there to teach them—just as we do not make our children; they are born to us. Subjectivity, therefore, is precisely *not* an outcome and even less a learning outcome; it is precisely *not* a thing that can be produced—which is why I like the idea of the *event* of subjectivity and of subjectivity-as-event so much. But it leads to a certain predicament for educators in that on the one hand I am arguing—and I am not alone in arguing this but am connecting to a long educational tradition—that the question of subjectivity should be a prime educational interest, whereas on the other hand I seem to be saying that there is nothing that educators can do.

My response to this predicament is to argue that while subjectivity cannot be *produced* through education—or for that matter politics—it is actually quite easy to *prevent* the event of subjectivity from occurring. If the event of subjectivity has to do with the ways in which I can be addressed by the other, by the otherness of the other, it is quite easy, both at the individual level and at the institutional level, to create situations in which the possibility for being addressed is edited out, where, as Jan Masschelein has put it, we become immunized for the call of the other, where we put up our fences, close our eyes and ears—and perhaps even our hearts—and eradicate the very risk of being interrupted by the other, the risk of being addressed by the other, of being put into question by the other, to use a Levinasian phrase. And that is perhaps the greatest problem with making education into a risk-free experience, into a zone where we can no longer be put into question, where we can no longer be addressed, where we can no longer be touched, where I am never at stake, so to speak. To make education 100 percent safe, to make it 100 percent risk-free, thus means that education becomes fundamentally uneducational. That is why the risk of education—what I tend to call the *beautiful* risk of education—is so very important; but I am aware that it is not fashionable to argue that education ought to be risky.

PW: Does that also lie behind your critique of certain tendencies in educational research? I'm thinking here, for example, of your critique of evidence-based education in your "Why 'What Works' Won't Work" essay (Biesta 2007b).

GB: Absolutely. The whole idea of evidence-based education is again based on the eradication of risk and a desire for total control over the educational process. There are a number of issues here. One has to do with the assumptions about educational processes and practices that inform the conception of research that is promoted here. The assumption is that education can be understood as a causal process—a process of production—and that the knowledge we need is about the causal connections between inputs and outcomes. I don't think that education is such a process—and I also don't think that education should be *understood* as such a process or, even worse, should be *modeled* as such a process. The latter point is important because I do think that it is, in principle, possible to model education as a causal process, that is, to make it into a process that operates in a causal way. This can be done by radically reducing the complexity of the educational process (Biesta 2010a). This requires that we control *all* the factors that potentially influence the connection between educational inputs and educational outcomes. This can be done, but it is a huge effort, which not only raises the question whether it's worth the effort—the Soviet Union wasn't able to sustain the total control of its citizens, and probably North Korea will not be able to sustain it in the end—and also whether the effort is desirable, and when you take it to its extremes it's quite obvious that the effort is ultimately not desirable. But it is a slippery slope, and in a lot of countries education is rapidly moving in this direction and is becoming oppressive, not only for those at the receiving end—students—but perhaps even more so for those who have to work under such oppressive conditions: teachers, school leaders, and administrators.

PW: Is there a risk that you create a rather black-and-white picture, where it is either control or freedom, either causality or total openness?

GB: That's a fair point, and it actually has to do with one of the things I realized after the publication of *Beyond Learning,* which is that while the question of subjectivity is a very important and, in a sense, both essential and fundamental dimension of education, it is not the be-all and end-all of education. That is why in my book *Good Education in an Age of Measurement* (Biesta 2010b) I argued that education, particularly school education, not only functions with regard to human subjectivity but performs other functions as well. In the book I refer to those other functions as qualification—this is the domain of knowledge, skills, and dispositions—and socialization—which I defined as the way in which, through education, we become part of existing "orders" (social orders, political orders, cultural orders, religious orders, professional orders, and so on). I think that it is important to be aware that education functions in these three domains. But I also see these three domains as three dimensions of educational purpose, that is, three dimensions in which educators can claim that education should function, should make an impact. Perhaps—but I still want to say this with great caution—questions about relationships between inputs and outcomes, questions about making education "work," have a place where it concerns the qualification and socialization dimension of education. After all, if we want our students to learn complex skills—like flying a Boeing 777, performing brain surgery, but actually in the whole domain of skills, including car mechanics, plumbing, et cetera—we want to make sure that our students get it "right" (which for me always also includes the need for students to be able to make judgments about what it means to get it right, plus the ability to judge when getting it right is not what is needed in a particular situation). So we have to be mindful that education is not just about the question of the subject. But at the same time I would also say that if this dimension falls out—if it disappears from the scene, if it is no longer considered to be relevant, then we have ended up in an *un*educational space. The art of teaching, in my view, is precisely that of finding the right balance among the three dimensions, and this is an ongoing task, not something that can be pre-programmed or sorted out by research.

PW: A final question then: what is the place of democracy in your theory of education?

GB: While in what I have said so far I haven't used the word *democracy* I hope that it is clear that there is a strong democratic "sentiment" in the way in which I look at education. For me it goes back to the connection between subjectivity-as-event and the idea that the event of subjectivity is only possible under the condition of plurality. That, in a sense, is where the democratic ethos and the educational ethos come together and perhaps even coincide. That is why, for me, the democratic is at the very heart of the educational—it's not an add-on, but it is what is at stake if we see the event of subjectivity in the way in which I have tried to approach it.

Bibliography

Andreotti, V. (2011). *Actionable postcolonial theory in education*. New York: Palgrave Macmillan.

Apple, M., and Beane, J. (1995). *Democratic schools*. Alexandria, VA: Association for Supervision and Curriculum Development.

Arendt, H. (1958). *The human condition*. Chicago: University of Chicago Press.

Arendt, H. (1977a). The crisis in education. In H. Arendt, *Between past and future: Eight exercises in political thought*. Harmondsworth: Penguin Books.

Arendt, H. (1977b). What is freedom? In H. Arendt, *Between past and future: Eight exercises in political thought*. Harmondsworth: Penguin Books.

Arendt, H. (1977c). Truth and politics. In H. Arendt, *Between past and future: Eight exercises in political thought*. Harmondsworth: Penguin Books.

Arendt, H. (1982). *Lectures on Kant's political philosophy*. Chicago: University of Chicago Press.

Arendt, H. (1994). Understanding and politics (the difficulties of understanding). In H. Arendt and J. Kohn (Eds.), *Essays in understanding 1930–1954*. New York: Harcourt, Brace and Company.

Arendt, H. (2003). "What remains? The language remains": A conversation with Günter Gaus. In P. Baher (Ed.), *The portable Hannah Arendt*. New York: Penguin Books.

Aristotle (1980). *The Nicomachean ethics*. Oxford: Oxford University Press.

Aspin, D. N., and Chapman, J. D. (2001). Lifelong learning: Concepts, theories and values. In *Proceedings of the 31st Annual Conference of SCUTREA*. University of East London: SCUTREA.

Barr, R. B., and Tagg, J. (1995). From teaching to learning: A new paradigm for undergraduate education. *Change* (November/December), 13–25.

Bauman, Z. (1993). *Postmodern ethics*. Oxford: Blackwell.

Bauman, Z. (1998). *Leven met veranderlijkheid, verscheidenheid en onzekerheid*. Amsterdam: Boom.

Bennington, G. (2000). *Interrupting Derrida*. London and New York: Routledge.

Biesta, G. J. J. (1994). Pragmatism as a pedagogy of communicative action. *Studies in Philosophy and Education, 13*(3–4), 273–290.

Biesta, G. J. J. (1998). "Say you want a revolution...." Suggestions for the impossible future of critical pedagogy. *Educational Theory, 48*(4), 499–510.

Biesta, G. J. J. (2001). "Preparing for the incalculable": Deconstruction, justice, and the question of education. In G. J. J. Biesta and D. Egéa-Kuehne (Eds.), *Derrida and education.* London and New York: Routledge.

Biesta, G. J. J. (2003). Jacques Derrida: Deconstruction = justice. In M. Peters, M. Olssen, and C. Lankshear (Eds.), *Futures of critical theory: Dreams of difference.* Lanham, MD: Rowman and Littlefield.

Biesta, G. J. J. (2004a). Education after deconstruction. In J. Marshall (Ed.), *Poststructuralism, philosophy, pedagogy.* Dordrecht and Boston: Kluwer Academic Press.

Biesta, G. (2004b). The community of those who have nothing in common: Education and the language of responsibility. *Interchange, 35*(3), 307–324.

Biesta, G. J. J. (2005). What can critical pedagogy learn from postmodernism? Further reflections on the impossible future of critical pedagogy. In I. Gur Ze'ev (Ed.), *Critical theory and critical pedagogy today: Toward a new critical language in education.* Haifa: University of Haifa.

Biesta, G. J. J. (2006a). *Beyond learning: Democratic education for a human future.* Boulder, CO: Paradigm Publishers.

Biesta, G. J. J. (2006b). "Of all affairs, communication is the most wonderful": Education as communicative praxis. In D. T. Hansen (Ed.), *John Dewey and our educational prospect: A critical engagement with Dewey's* democracy and education. Albany, NY: SUNY Press.

Biesta, G. J. J. (2006c). What's the point of lifelong learning if lifelong learning has no point? On the democratic deficit of policies for lifelong learning. *European Educational Research Journal, 5*(3–4), 169–180.

Biesta, G. J. J. (2007a). Education and the democratic person: Towards a political understanding of democratic education. *Teachers College Record, 109*(3), 740–769.

Biesta, G. J. J. (2007b). Why "what works" won't work: Evidence-based practice and the democratic deficit of educational research. *Educational Theory, 57*(1), 1–22.

Biesta, G. J. J. (2008). Pedagogy with empty hands: Levinas, education, and the question of being human. In D. Egéa-Kuehne (Ed.), *Levinas and education: At the intersection of faith and reason.* London and New York: Routledge.

Biesta, G. J. J. (2009). Good education in an age of measurement: On the need to reconnect with the question of purpose in education. *Educational Assessment, Evaluation, and Accountability, 21*(1), 33–46.

Biesta, G. J. J. (2010a). Five theses on complexity reduction and its politics. In D. C. Osberg and G. J. J. Biesta (Eds.), *Complexity theory and the politics of education.* Rotterdam: Sense Publishers.

Biesta, G. J. J. (2010b). *Good education in an age of measurement: Ethics, politics, democracy.* Boulder, CO: Paradigm Publishers.

Biesta, G. J. J. (2010c). Why "what works" still won't work: From evidence-based education to value-based education. *Studies in Philosophy and Education, 29*(5), 491–503.

Biesta, G. J. J. (2010d). Evidenz und Werte in Erziehung und Bildung: Drei weitere Defizite evidenzbasierter Praxis. In H.-U. Otto, A. Polutta, and H. Ziegler

(Hrsg.), *What works—Welches Wissen braucht die Soziale Arbeit?* Opladen, Germany: Barbara Burdich.

Biesta, G. J. J. (2010e). How to exist politically and learn from it: Hannah Arendt and the problem of democratic education. *Teachers College Record, 112*(2), 558–577.

Biesta, G. J. J. (2011a). Disciplines and theory in the academic study of education: A comparative analysis of the Anglo-American and Continental construction of the field. *Pedagogy, Culture, and Society, 19*(2), 175–192.

Biesta, G. J. J. (2011b). *Learning democracy in school and society.* Rotterdam/Boston/Taipei: Sense Publishers.

Biesta, G. J. J., and Egéa-Kuehne, D. (Eds.) (2001). *Derrida and education.* London and New York: Routledge.

Biesta, G. J. J., and Lawy, R. (2006). From teaching citizenship to learning democracy. *Cambridge Journal of Education, 36*(1), 63–79.

Bingham, C. (2009). *Authority is relational.* Albany, NY: SUNY Press.

Bingham, C., and Biesta, G. J. J. (2010). *Jacques Rancière: Education, truth, emancipation.* London and New York: Continuum.

Boyne, R. (1990). *Foucault and Derrida: The other side of reason.* London: Routledge.

Brackertz, N. (2007). *Who is hard to reach and why?* Institute of Social Research Working Paper. Melbourne: Swinburne University of Technology.

Britzman, D. (1998). *Lost subjects, contested objects: Toward a psychoanalytic inquiry of learning.* Albany, NY: SUNY Press.

Caputo, J. D. (Ed.). (1997). *Deconstruction in a nutshell. A conversation with Jacques Derrida.* New York: Fordham University Press.

Caputo, J. D. (2006). *The weakness of God: A theology of the event.* Bloomington and Indianapolis: Indiana University Press.

Caputo, J. D. (2007). *How to read Kierkegaard.* London: Granta Books.

Caputo, J. D., and Vattimo, G. (2007). *After the death of God.* New York: Columbia University Press.

Carr, W. (1987). What is an educational practice? *Journal of Philosophy of Education, 21*(2), 163–175.

Critchley, S. (1999). *Ethics—politics—subjectivity: Essays on Derrida, Levinas, and contemporary French thought.* London: Verso.

Deakin Crick, R. (2008). Key competencies for education in a European context. *European Educational Research Journal, 7*(3), 311–318.

Delors, J., et al. (1996). *Learning: The treasure within.* Paris: UNESCO.

Department for Education and Employment (1998). The learning age: A renaissance for a new Britain. London: The Stationery Office.

Derrida, J. (1978). *Writing and difference.* Chicago: University of Chicago Press.

Derrida, J. (1982). *Margins of philosophy.* Chicago: University of Chicago Press.

Derrida, J. (1984). Deconstruction and the other: An interview with Jacques Derrida. In R. Kearney, *Dialogues with contemporary Continental thinkers.* Manchester, UK: Manchester University Press.

Derrida, J. (1991). Letter to a Japanese friend. In P. Kamuf (Ed.), *A Derrida reader: Between the blinds* (pp. 270–276). New York: Columbia University Press.

Derrida, J. (1992a). *Given time: I. Counterfeit money,* trans. Peggy Kamuf. Chicago: University of Chicago Press.

Derrida. J. (1992b). Force of law: The "mystical foundation of authority." In D. Cornell, M. Rosenfeld, and D. Carlson (Eds.), *Deconstruction and the possibility of justice.* New York and London: Routledge.

Derrida, J. (1994). *Specters of Marx.* New York: Routledge.

Derrida, J. (1997). The Villanova roundtable: A conversation with Jacques Derrida. In J. D. Caputo (Ed.), *Deconstruction in a nutshell: A conversation with Jacques Derrida.* New York: Fordham University Press.

Derrida, J. (2001). "I have a taste for the secret." In J. Derrida and M. Ferraris, *A taste for the secret.* Cambridge: Polity Press.

Derrida, J., and Ewald, F. (2001). "A certain 'madness' must watch over thinking." Jacques Derrida's interview with François Ewald, trans. Denise Egéa-Kuehne. In G. J. J. Biesta and D. Egéa-Kuehne (Eds.), *Derrida and education.* London and New York: Routledge.

Dewey, J. (1895). *Plan of organization of the university primary school.* In J. A. Boydston (Ed.), *John Dewey, The early works, 1882–1898. Volume 5.* Carbondale and Edwardsville: Southern Illinois University Press.

Dewey, J. (1897). *My pedagogic creed.* In J. A. Boydston (Ed.), *John Dewey, The early works, 1882–1898. Volume 5.* Carbondale and Edwardsville: Southern Illinois University Press.

Dewey, J. (1916). *Democracy and education.* In J. A. Boydston (Ed.), *John Dewey, The middle works, 1899–1924. Volume 9.* Carbondale and Edwardsville: Southern Illinois University Press.

Dewey, J. (1958 [1929]). *Experience and nature. Second edition.* New York: Dover.

Disch, L. J. (1994). *Hannah Arendt and the limits of philosophy.* Ithaca, NY, and London: Cornell University Press.

Eagleton, T. (2007). *Ideology: An introduction. New and updated edition.* London and New York: Verso.

Egéa-Kuehne, D. (Ed.). (2008). *Levinas and education: At the intersection of faith and reason.* London and New York: Routledge.

ELLI Development Team (2008). *European Lifelong Learning Indicators: Developing a conceptual framework.* Gütersloh, Germany: Bertelsmann Stiftung.

Eraut, M. (2003). National vocational qualifications in England: Description and analysis of an alternative qualification system. In G. Straka (Ed.), *Zertifizierung non-formell und informell erworbener beruflicher Kompetenzen.* Münster/New York: Waxmann.

Faure, E., et al. (1972). *Learning to be: The world of education today and tomorrow.* Paris: UNESCO.

Fejes, A. (2006). *Constructing the adult learner: A governmentality analysis.* Linköping, Sweden: Linköping University.

Festenstein, M. (1997). *Pragmatism and political theory: From Dewey to Rorty.* Chicago: University of Chicago Press.

Field, J. (2000). *Lifelong learning and the new educational order.* Stoke-on-Trent, UK: Trentham.

Forneck, H. J., and Wrana, D. (2005). Transformationen des Feldes der Weiterbildung. In H. J. Forneck and D. Wrana (Eds.), *Ein parzelliertes Field: Eine Einführung in die Erwachsenenbildung.* Bielefeld, Germany: Bertelsmann.

Foucault, M. (1975). *Discipline and punish: The birth of the prison.* New York: Vintage.

Foucault, M. (1977). A preface to transgression. In D. F. Bouchard (Ed.), *Language, counter-memory, practice: Selected essays and an interview by Michel Foucault.* Ithaca, NY: Cornell University Press.

Foucault, M. (1984). What is enlightenment? In P. Rabinow (Ed.), *The Foucault reader.* New York: Pantheon.

Foucault, M. (1991). Questions of method. In G. Burchell, C. Gordon, and P. Miller (Eds.), *The Foucault effect: Studies in governmentality.* Chicago: University of Chicago Press.

Freire, P. (1972). Pedagogy of the oppressed. London: Penguin Books.

Garrison, J. (1999). John Dewey, Jacques Derrida, and the metaphysics of presence. *Transactions of the Charles S. Peirce Society, 35*(2), 346–372.

Gordon, M. (1999). Hannah Arendt on authority: Conservativism in education reconsidered. *Educational Theory, 49*(2), 161–180.

Gordon, M. (Ed.). (2002). *Hannah Arendt and education: Renewing our common world.* Boulder, CO: Westview Press, 2002.

Gough, N. (2010). Can we escape the program? Inventing possible/impossible futures in/for Australian educational research. *Australian Educational Researcher, 37*(4), 9–32.

Green, B. (2010). The (im)possibility of the project. *Australian Educational Researcher, 37*(3), 1–17.

Gur Ze'ev, I. (Ed.). (2005). *Critical theory and critical pedagogy today: Toward a new critical language in education.* Haifa: University of Haifa.

Habermas, J. (1987). *The theory of communicative action. Volume two: Lifeword and system: A critique of functionalist reason.* Boston: Beacon Press.

Habermas, J. (1990). *The philosophical discourse of modernity.* Cambridge, MA: MIT Press.

Hansen, P. (2005). Hannah Arendt and bearing with strangers. *Contemporary Political Theory, 3,* 3–22.

Heller, Á., and Fehér, F. (1989). *The postmodern political condition.* New York: Columbia University Press.

Henriksen, J.-O. (2010). Thematizing otherness: On ways of conceptualizing transcendence and God in recent philosophy of religion. *Studia Theologica—Nordic Journal of Theology, 64*(2), 153–176.

James, W. (1899). *Talks to teachers on psychology: And to students on some of life's ideals.* New York: Henry Holt and Company.

Kant, I. (1982). Über Pädagogik [On education]. In I. Kant, *Schriften zur Anthropologie, Geschichtsphilosophie, Politik und Pädagogik.* Frankfurt am Main: Insel Verlag.

Kant, I. (1992 [1784]). An answer to the question "what is enlightenment?" In P. Waugh (Ed.), *Post-modernism: A reader* (pp. 89–95). London: Edward Arnold.

Kerr, D. (2005). Citizenship education in England—listening to young people: New insights from the citizenship education longitudinal study. *International Journal of Citizenship and Teacher Education, 1*(1), 74–96.

Kierkegaard, S. (1985). *Philosophical fragments.* In H. V. Hong and E. H. Hong (Eds. and Trans.), *Kierkegaard's writings VII.* Princeton, NJ: Princeton University Press.

Kierkegaard, S. (1992). *Concluding unscientific postscript to philosophical fragments, Volume 1.* In H. V. Hong and E. H. Hong (Eds. and Trans.), *Kierkegaard's writings XII.* Princeton, NJ: Princeton University Press.

Kierkegaard, S. (1996). *Papers and journals: A selection.* London and New York: Penguin Books.

Lave, J., and Wenger, E. (1991). *Situated learning: Legitimate peripheral participation.* Cambridge: Cambridge University Press.

Leeming, D. A. (2010). *Creation myths of the world. Second edition.* Santa Barbara, CA: ABC-CLIO/Greenwood.

Levinas, E. (1969). *Totality and infinity: An essay on exteriority.* Pittsburgh: Duquesne University Press.

Levinas, E. (1981). *Otherwise than being or beyond essence.* The Hague: Martinus Nijhoff.

Levinas, E. (1985). *Ethics and infinity.* Pittsburgh: Duquesne University Press.

Levinas, E. (1987). Phenomenon and enigma. In E. Levinas, *Collected philosophical papers.* Dordrecht: Nijhoff.

Levinas, E. (1989). Ethics as first philosophy. In S. Hand (Ed.), *The Levinas reader.* Oxford: Blackwell.

Levinas, E. (1998a). *Entre-nous: On thinking-of-the-Other.* New York: Columbia University Press.

Levinas, E. (1998b). *Of God who comes to mind.* Stanford, CA: Stanford University Press.

Lingis, A. (1981). Translator's introduction. In E. Levinas, *Otherwise than being or beyond essence.* The Hague: Martinus Nijhoff.

Lucy, N. (2004). *A Derrida dictionary.* Oxford: Blackwell.

McLaren, P. (1997). *Revolutionary multiculturalism: Pedagogies of dissent for the new millennium.* Boulder, CO: Westview Press.

Meirieu, P. (2007). *Pédagogie: Le devoir de résister.* Issy-les-Moulineaux, France: ESF éditeur.

Meirieu, P. (2008). Le maître, serviteur public. Sur quoi fonder l'autorité des enseignants dans nos sociétés démocratiques? Conférence donnée dans le cadre de l'École d'été de Rosa Sensat, Université de Barcelone, juillet 2008. Retrieved from www.meirieu.com/ARTICLES/maitre_serviteur_public_version2.pdf (June 1, 2012).

Messerschmidt, A. (2011). Weiter bilden? Anmerkungen zum lebenslangen Lernen aus erwachsenenbildnerischer und bildunstheoretischer Perspektive, in Kommision Sozialpädagogik (Ed.), *Bildung des Effective Citizen: Sozialpädagogik auf dem Weg zu einem neuen Sozialentwurf.* Weinheim/München: Juventa.

Miedema, S., and Biesta, G. J. J. (2004). Jacques Derrida's religion with/out religion and the im/possibility of religious education. *Religious Education, 99*(1), 23–37.

Mollenhauer, K. (1976). *Erziehung und emanzipation.* München: Juventa.

Mulder, M., Weigel, T., and Collins, K. (2007). The concept of competence concept in the development of vocational education and training in selected EU member states: A critical analysis. *Journal of Vocational Education and Training, 59*(1), 65–85.

Neil, A. S. (1966). *Freedom—Not license!* New York: Hart.

Nola, R., and Irzik, G. (2005). Philosophy, science, education, and culture. Dordrecht: Springer.

O'Bryne, A. (2005). Pedagogy without a project: Arendt and Derrida on teaching, responsibility, and revolution. *Studies in Philosophy and Education, 24*(5), 389–409.

Organisation for Economic Co-operation and Development (OECD) (1973). *Recurrent education: A strategy for lifelong learning*. Paris: OECD.

Organisation for Economic Co-operation and Development (1997). *Lifelong learning for all*. Paris: OECD.

Papastephanou, M. (2012). Crossing the divide within Continental philosophy: Reconstruction, deconstruction, dialogue, and education. *Studies in Philosophy and Education, 31*(2), 153–170.

Pelletier, C. (2009). Emancipation, equality, and education: Rancière's critique of Bourdieu and the question of performativity. *Discourse, 30*(2), 137–159.

Pols, W. (2001). Voorbij de pedagogiek van de regel [Beyond the education of the rule]. *Pedagogiek, 21*(3), 195–199.

Rancière, J. (1991a). *The ignorant schoolmaster: Five lessons in intellectual emancipation*. Stanford, CA: Stanford University Press.

Rancière, J. (1991b). *The nights of labor*. Philadelphia: Temple University Press.

Rancière, J. (1995). *On the shores of politics*. London and New York: Verso.

Rancière, J. (1999). *Dis-agreement: Politics and philosophy*. Minneapolis: University of Minnesota Press.

Rancière, J. (2003). *The philosopher and his poor*. Durham, NC, and London: Duke University Press.

Rancière, J. (2004). *The politics of aesthetics*. London: Continuum.

Rancière, J. (2009). A few remarks on the methods of Jacques Rancière. *Parallax, 15*(3), 114–123.

Rancière, J. (2010). On ignorant schoolmasters. In C. Bingham and G. J. J. Biesta, *Jacques Rancière: Education, truth, emancipation*. London and New York: Continuum.

Rancière, J., Panagia, D., and Bowlby, R. (2001). Ten theses on politics. *Theory and Event, 5*(3).

Richardson, V. (2003). Constructivist pedagogy. *Teachers College Record, 105*(9), 1623–1640.

Roth, W.-M. (2011). *Passability: At the limits of the constructivist metaphor*. Dordrecht: Springer.

Ruitenberg, C. (2011). The empty chair: Education in an ethic of hospitality. In R. Kunzman (Ed.), *Philosophy of Education 2011*. Urbana-Champaign, IL: Philosophy of Education Society.

Sæverot, H. (2011). Kierkegaard, seduction, and existential education. *Studies in Philosophy and Education, 30*(6), 557–572.

Schutz, A. (2002). Is political education an oxymoron? Hannah Arendt's resistance to public spaces in schools. Philosophy of Education 2001. Urbana-Champaign, IL: Philosophy of Education Society.

Simons, J. (1995). *Foucault and the political*. London and New York: Routledge.

Simons, M., and Masschelein, J. (2009). Our will to learn and the assemblage of a learning apparatus. In A. Fejes and K. Nicoll (Eds.), *Foucault and lifelong learning*. London and New York: Routledge.

Sleeper, R. W. (1986). *The necessity of pragmatism*. New Haven, CT: Yale University Press.

Stengel, B., and Weems, L. (2010). Questioning safe space: An introduction. *Studies in Philosophy and Education, 29*(6), 505–507.

Tenorth, H.-E. (2008 [2003]). *Geschichte der Erziehung: Einführung in die Grundzüge ihrer neuzeitlichen Entwicklung.* Munchen: Weinheim.

Todd, S. (2003). *Learning from the other.* Albany, NY: SUNY Press.

Vanderstraeten, R., and Biesta, G. J. J. (2001). How is education possible? *Educational Philosophy and Theory, 33*(1), 7–21.

Vanderstraeten, R., and Biesta, G. J. J. (2006). How is education possible? A pragmatist account of communication and the social organisation of education. *British Journal of Educational Studies, 54*(2), 160–174.

Westphal, M. (2008). *Levinas and Kierkegaard in dialogue.* Bloomington and Indianapolis: Indiana University Press.

Winter, P. (2011). Coming into the world, uniqueness, and the beautiful risk of education: An interview with Gert Biesta by Philip Winter. *Studies in Philosophy and Education, 30*(5): 537–542.

Yang, J., and Valdés-Cotera, R. (Eds.) (2011). *Conceptual evolution and policy developments in lifelong learning.* Hamburg: UNESCO Institute for Lifelong Learning.

Yeaxlee, B. A. (1929). *Lifelong education.* London: Casell.

Sources to Be Acknowledged

Chapter 1 is partly based on Biesta, G. J. J. (2009), "The weakness of education: For a pedagogy of the event," a paper presented at the annual meeting of the American Educational Research Association, San Diego, CA, April 13–17, 2009. The idea of a Levinasian pedagogy with empty hands was first developed in Biesta, G. J. J. (2008), "Pedagogy with empty hands: Levinas, education, and the question of being human," in D. Egéa-Kuehne (Ed.), *Levinas and education: At the intersection of faith and reason* (London and New York: Routledge). The idea of deconstructive pragmatism in Chapter 2 was first developed in Biesta, G. J. J. (2010), "'This is my truth, tell me yours': Deconstructive pragmatism as a philosophy for education," *Educational Philosophy and Theory, 42*(7), 710–727. Chapter 3 is based on Biesta, G. J. J. (2013), "Receiving the gift of teaching: From 'learning from' to 'being taught by,'" *Studies in Philosophy and Education.* Chapter 4 originates from a keynote presentation at the Discourse, Power, and Resistance Conference in Plymouth, UK, in 2012. Chapter 5 makes use of Biesta, G. J. J. (2010), "A new 'logic' of emancipation: The methodology of Jacques Rancière," *Educational Theory, 60*(1), 39–59; and Chapter 6 of Biesta, G. J. J. (2010), "How to exist politically and learn from it: Hannah Arendt and the problem of democratic education," *Teachers College Record, 112*(2), 558–577. Chapter 7 is based on an invited keynote presentation at the 2020: The Future of Teacher Education Conference in Vienna in 2011. The interview in the appendix appeared in *Studies in Philosophy and Education, 30*(5), 537–542.

Index

About the Author

Gert J. J. Biesta (www.gertbiesta.com) is Professor of Educational Theory and Policy at the University of Luxembourg, former president of the Philosophy of Education Society USA, and editor-in-chief of the journal *Studies in Philosophy and Education*. With Paradigm Publishers he has published *Beyond Learning: Democratic Education for a Human Future* (2006)—winner of the 2008 American Educational Studies Association Critics' Choice Book Award—and *Good Education in an Age of Measurement: Ethics, Politics, Democracy* (2010). He also co-edited George Herbert Mead's *The Philosophy of Education* (2008).